HOW TO
INTERVIEW
LIKE A TOP
MBA

Job-Winning Strategies from Headhunters, Fortune 100 Recruiters, and Career Counselors

DR. SHEL LEANNE

McGraw·Hill

New York   Chicago   San Francisco   Lisbon   London   Madrid   Mexico City
Milan   New Delhi   San Juan   Seoul   Singapore   Sydney   Toronto

Library of Congress Cataloging-in-Publication Data

Leanne, Shelly.
     How to interview like a top MBA : job-winning strategies from headhunters,
    Fortune 100 recruiters, and career counselors / by Shelly Leanne.
         p.   cm.
     Includes index.
     ISBN 0-07-141827-X (alk. paper)
     1. Employment interviewing.   2. Job hunting.   II. Title.

HF5549.5.I6L42   2004
650.14′4—dc22   2003023695

   10 11 12 13 14 15 16 17 18 19 20 21 22   FGR/FGR   0 9 8 7

ISBN-13:978-0-07-141827-0
ISBN-10:   0-07-141827-X

McGraw-Hill books are available at special quantity discounts to use as premiums and sales promotions, or for use in corporate training programs. For more information, please write to the Director of Special Sales, Professional Publishing, McGraw-Hill, Two Penn Plaza, New York, NY 10121-2298. Or contact your local bookstore.

This publication is designed to provide information about preparing for interviews but provides no guarantees or warranties about interview outcomes. For privacy purposes, fictitious names are used in place of the real names of some of the Fortune 100 professionals, career counselors, and other corporate personnel who contributed insights to this book.

This book is printed on acid-free paper.

CONTENTS

PREFACE

O ver the years, I have benefited from outstanding academic and career advice and from excellent mentoring and interview coaching. Many of my successes—from gaining admission to top universities, to landing jobs within prestigious companies such as McKinsey & Company and Morgan Stanley—would not have been possible except for the wonderful mentoring I have received over the years. My gratitude for this assistance created in me years ago a dedication to empowering other people with knowledge and resources, helping enable them to make their own dreams become reality. For more than fifteen years, I have developed my own perspectives on interviewing and career management best practices, and I have conveyed those perspectives to others, helping them to secure access to excellent jobs and academic programs as a result. I have enjoyed designing educational resources using different tools that prod people to think deeply about how they can best develop their talents, how they can put them to use, and how they can effectively draw on educational resources to open doors of opportunity.

In this work, I am happy to share important insights about interviewing. The art of interviewing excellently is relevant not only for those in business, but for those pursuing employment in many other fields—from law to the nonprofit sector. Similarly, the insights of this book can help you regardless of whether you are seeking full-time employment, part-time employment, internships, or admission into academic programs.

In the past, I have enjoyed serving as an interview coach to students at Harvard College, the Harvard Kennedy School of Government, and Harvard Business School. I have equally enjoyed witnessing the impact that interview coaching can bring, as I have watched those students gain access to top graduate schools such as Harvard, Stanford, Yale, and Columbia, and top companies such as McKinsey & Company and Goldman Sachs. As one student commented after gaining admission to Columbia University's Graduate School of Business, "The admissions interviewer actually told me before we finished that he was very impressed by my answers!"

Indeed, when it comes to interviewing, delivery is key—in terms of your résumé presentation, and in terms of your interactions with the interviewer before, during, and after the interview. It is not merely your qualifications that matter, but how you communicate your qualifications, and whether you effectively portray yourself as an excellent choice and a wonderful fit for the job or opportunity at hand. Those who know how to interview excellently generally fare better in securing job interviews, internships, scholarships, or admission to competitive academic programs. When you have become adept at communicating your qualifications and candidacy in compelling terms and promoting yourself in ways that will make the interviewer see you as the ideal candidate, you are likely to be pleased more often with your interview outcomes.

I hope this work will help provide you with knowledge and best practices that empower you in the interviewing process. By coming to understand the underlying purpose of questions posed and how to present your qualifications in the most compelling light, it is my hope you will learn how to interview excellently.

In this book, I draw on input from professionals who are or have been engaged in recruiting efforts at Fortune 100 and other top companies such as IBM, Procter & Gamble, J. P. Morgan Chase, Verizon, American Express, Cisco Systems, Intel, Lucent Technologies, Staples, Prudential, Oracle, Smith Barney Citigroup, McKinsey & Company, Morgan Stanley, Goldman Sachs, Ernst & Young, and PricewaterhouseCoopers. I must thank the Fortune 100 and other corporate executives for sharing their insights with me. I must also thank those corporate executives, executive recruiters, and career counselors who took the time to allow me to interview them, so that we could include their insights directly in this book. I hope you enjoy the excerpts from my conversations with them, which are woven throughout this text.

I thank Wilbert Watts, Jr., my wonderful husband and best friend, for his love and encouragement. I thank my family, the Geigers and the Holloways, for their years of dedication and support. Thank you in particular to Aunt Mildred Geiger, Uncle William Geiger, Aunt Ann Lewis, Uncle Alonzo Lewis, Uncle Edward Geiger, and my lovely brother David Geiger, Jr. I express gratitude to Christine Baker, formerly of the Harvard Bureau of Study Counsel, for years of excellent mentoring. Thank you to Lorelee Parker and Julie Taylor, two wonderful friends. Thank you to Sponsors for Educational Opportunity for their excellent work. I express my deep appreciation to Nina Graybill, my literary lawyer, for her steadfast support and insightful advice. I give a hearty thank-you to my editor, Mary Glenn, who was so dedicated and encouraging throughout the entire editing process. A big thank-you also to Nancy Hall, my project editor, who provided excellent work and support, which helped bring this book to fruition.

INTRODUCTION

In today's business world, competition for jobs has never been keener. Rather than keeping the same job for twenty years, a worker typically changes jobs at least five times in a lifetime. In addition, the pool of job applicants is seemingly expanding, as companies have come to recognize the value that nontraditional candidates (engineers, lawyers, health care professionals, and the like) can bring to general management positions. Responding to this highly competitive environment, top U.S. business schools have intensified the preparation they provide their MBA students who are seeking full-time employment. Students are exposed to guest lecturers, benefit from private coaches, and receive videotaped mock interviews to give them detailed feedback and coaching. These efforts enable MBA graduates from top U.S. programs to fine-tune their responses to tough questions in job interviews.

Overall, headhunters agree that in recent years, attractive candidates for competitive jobs have developed a much more refined approach to interviewing than past applicants. Recognizing these trends, *How to Interview Like a Top MBA: Job-Winning Strategies from Headhunters, Fortune 100 Recruiters, and Career Counselors* introduces you to some "best practice" interviewing techniques. Whether you are seeking your first full-time employment, switching jobs, applying for a part-time job, or preparing for graduate school admission interviews, this book introduces you to approaches that can sharpen the delivery of your interview. The insights in this book can be helpful not only for business interviews, but also for candidates in other fields from law to the non-profit sector.

The best practices highlighted in this book are garnered from four main sources. I introduce best practices and advice based upon my years of experience as a Fortune 100 professional, strategic adviser, and career counselor. In addition, I draw on input from professionals who are or have been engaged in recruiting efforts at companies such as IBM, Procter & Gamble, J. P. Morgan Chase, Verizon, American Express, Cisco Systems, Intel, Lucent Technologies, Staples, Prudential, Oracle, Salomon Brothers, Morgan Stanley, Goldman Sachs, McKinsey & Company, Ernst & Young, and PricewaterhouseCoopers, among others. My work with MBA students at Harvard, Wharton, Columbia, Cornell, Yale, and MIT has also informed the writing of this work, as have my conversations with executive recruiters ("headhunters") from such institutions as Berkhemer Clayton and Garb Jaffe and Associates.

Ten Common Interview Mistakes

Based upon my experience and many conversations with Fortune 100 recruiters, headhunters, and career counselors, I have been struck by the pronounced themes that have emerged about the common mistakes candidates make during job interviews. The ten common interview mistakes were easily identifiable. Among these were the failure to create a positive first impression and the inability to communicate the relevance of one's professional experience to the job offered. Effective interview preparation seeks to address these common mistakes. Thus, this book is organized around these ten common mistakes and is structured to convey best practices, helping you learn how to employ the best practices of excellent interviewing.

Top Ten Interview Mistakes
   1. Failed to make a great first impression
      - Treated informal interviews carelessly
      - Dressed poorly
      - Ignored business etiquette
      - Failed to demonstrate enthusiasm

2. Did not appear versed in the basics about the company, industry, available job, or interviewer
3. Failed to present an effective résumé
   - Didn't have a strong story line
   - Failed to articulate value of work experience or skills
   - Failed to back up claims on résumé
4. Failed to demonstrate a fit for the position
   - Unable to communicate the relevance of education or professional experience to the job available
   - Unable to communicate a fit with the culture of the company
5. Had inadequate answers to common, open-ended or "turnaround" questions
6. Failed to adequately address concerns about clear weaknesses
7. Did not satisfactorily explain periods of unemployment
8. Couldn't explain the relevance of "nontraditional" work experience to the available job (in the case of nontraditional candidates)
9. Asked disturbing question(s) at the end of the interview
10. Didn't leave a positive lasting impression

Best Practices

To address these common mistakes and introduce you to best practices, this book is divided into two parts. Part I provides ten chapters centered around best practices, to help you address the top ten mistakes associated with job interviewing. These chapters explain how to approach the interview and sharpen your delivery. They include practical advice, anecdotal examples, details about useful techniques, examples of interviewing success factors, and work sheets to help you map your own approach to your job interview.

Chapter 1, centering around the best practice "Create a Great First Impression," addresses the most common mistakes interviewees make—failing to dress well, ignoring key business etiquette, and treating an informal interview too casually. The chapter also provides techniques and tips you can employ to help create a great first impression.

Chapter 2, centers on the best practice "Do Your Homework in Four Key Areas," and addresses another common mistake: a candidate's failure to appear versed in the basic facts about the interviewing company, industry, advertised job, and interviewer(s). This chapter explains what sorts of information you should research in each of those four key areas before your interview. It also points you to resources to explore as you gather the information you need to sound informed and prepared during the interview. Chapter 2 explains how learning information in the four key areas can help you address common interview questions such as, "Why do you want to work for our company and not for our main competitor?"

Chapter 3, "Use Your Résumé as an Effective Interviewing Tool," addresses how you can avoid a situation in which you fail to make sense of your education and career moves to date. It helps you understand how to use your résumé as an effective tool in the interviewing process, tailoring your résumé specifically to the advertised job, highlighting the most attractive and relevant aspects of your work experience and educational history. It also helps you understand how to highlight transferable skills and employ résumé language that can help demonstrate a match between your qualifications and those of an ideal candidate.

Chapter 4, "Demonstrate a Fit Through Your Responses to Key Questions," illuminates how you can convey the relevance of your education and experience to the job for which you are interviewing. It helps pinpoint the aspects of your record you should emphasize when responding to questions about such things as your choice of career, work experience, and personality.

Chapter 5, "Shape the Interview with Responses to Open-Ended and Turnaround Questions," addresses how to use broad, general, or open-ended questions as chances to paint yourself in the most positive light and in a way that conveys a match with the job you are interviewing for. It also elaborates on how to "turn around" tricky questions like "Tell me about a professional failure," using such questions to underscore your winning attributes and accomplishments.

Chapter 6, "Address Clear Weaknesses (Without Apologizing!),"
presents techniques through which you can effectively address aspects
of your record that might cause concern for the interviewer. Weaknesses
in your record do not need to prevent you from securing a job if you
are able to address your concerns about them in a compelling and convincing manner.

Chapter 7, "Present a Strong Explanation if You've Been out of
Work," explains ways in which you can present periods of long unemployment in the most positive light, helping to create an image of yourself as a proactive professional dedicated to self-improvement and
professional development.

Chapter 8, "Demonstrate Business Relevance if You're a Nontraditional Hire," helps nontraditional candidates (candidates without business backgrounds, such as engineers, lawyers, artists, and the like)
understand how to demonstrate the relevance of their education and
skills to the job they are interviewing for. Here, the concept of transferable skills is key. The information in this chapter helps you identify
and highlight transferable skills.

Chapter 9, "End Your Interview Excellently," helps you to identify
how to end your interview so that it reinforces a positive impression,
through excellent closing comments or well-considered questions.

Chapter 10, "Follow Up, Reinforcing a Positive, Lasting Impression,"
provides ideas for how you can follow up an interview in ways that help
ensure the interviewer remembers you and has a favorable impression
of you.

100 Sample Questions and Answers

Part II provides 100 interview questions and sample answers in key categories, with critiques of the responses and information about what you
should avoid when responding to some of those questions. Specifically,
the structure of a Q&A section includes the following elements:

- Question and explanation of what the interviewer is likely looking
  for when asking the question

- Sample answer
- Analysis of answer
- Advice about what to avoid as you respond

The best practices presented in Chapters 1 through 10, the annotated examples, and the work sheets for developing your own action plan, together with the 100 sample questions and answers, can help you understand how to interview like a top MBA.

PART I

BEST PRACTICES

CHAPTER 1

CREATE A GREAT FIRST IMPRESSION

Headhunters, career counselors, and professionals engaged in recruiting efforts at Fortune 100 companies all stress the prime importance of creating a great first impression. As the old saying goes, you only make a first impression once, so you want to make sure that impression is excellent. The following aspects of making a great first impression stand out as most important.

"Informational" Interviews: Formal or Not, They're Interviews

Many candidates try to get an edge by securing informational interviews with human resources personnel or with professionals in the corporations in which they hope to gain employment. Others receive invitations to attend large informational sessions with corporate representatives to learn more about a particular company. Believing that the exchange will be informational and therefore informal, some candidates make the mistake of going into such situations too casually—unrehearsed, underdressed, unprepared for deep discussion because they have not adequately researched the industry and company, and inattentive to key business etiquette. Unwittingly, those candidates are making their first impression, and that first impression is largely negative. Headhunters, recruiters, and career counselors affirm that lack of preparedness for informal interviews can be a key reason as to why candidates lose job opportunities.

Therefore, pay attention to a little-known fact: During "informational" or "informal" interview sessions, many top companies actively evaluate candidates in the same way they would evaluate candidates during a formal interview. You are being observed, and corporate representatives often are taking mental notes. Following an informal session, many company representatives compile written notes about their exchange with you and disseminate them to other firm members. While I was working in corporate America, for instance, I attended an informational luncheon for Harvard Business School students, who had been invited to the large informal luncheon to meet members of our firm and learn more about our company. Little did the Harvard students realize, they were being evaluated, even down to their dining etiquette. After this informal session, many of the students were eliminated from consideration for formal interviews.

Consider the case of Jennifer. She attended this informal luncheon casually dressed, which might not have been a problem except that her clothing seemed to clash and did not seem well picked for the occasion. She chatted on before a group of corporate representatives, eating with poor etiquette, and laughing boisterously at questionable jokes she was making in front of one of the firm's partners. During the transition from casual mingling to the sit-down portion of the luncheon, Jennifer sat near corporate representatives and spoke in an unguarded way about her dislike of her undergraduate institution. I could see one of the partners wincing at her attitude and her poor table manners. The next morning, when I met with several corporate members to review the notes they had compiled about each candidate they had met, one partner summarized his opinion about Jennifer in three sentences: "She's boisterous, unmannerly, and has poor conversational skills. I certainly could never see any of us putting her in front of a client. She should not be granted a formal interview." Jennifer would perhaps never understand why she was not called for a formal interview, even though her performance in business school merited at least an initial formal interview. Unknowingly, she had had her first interview in an informal setting, and the lasting impression she made was universally negative.

Regardless of whether a session is called "informational," "informal," or "formal," therefore, you should err on the side of caution and assume you are being evaluated. The following guidelines for creating a great first impression therefore apply to each of these situations.

Dress the Part

An important way to create a great first impression is to dress well. These days, however, it is sometimes unclear what that means. For instance, if a company's dress code is "business casual" and you are going to interview there, should you dress in sharp business casual attire or in a suit? Consider these guidelines:

Suit or No Suit?

- If the company's professional employees dress in suits for their everyday in-office work, even when clients are *not* present, then you should wear a suit for any interview, unless instructed otherwise.
- If the company's professional employees dress in suits only when meeting with clients, but wear business casual for their everyday in-office work when clients are not present, then you should likely wear a suit for any interview, unless instructed otherwise.
- If the company's professional employees dress in business casual *both* when meeting with clients as well as for their everyday in-office work when clients are not present, that situation is much more tricky. Here, you might choose to dress in sharp business casual; that is, consider wearing a jacket to add a slightly formal touch to your business attire. However, it is always best to call a representative in human resources to ask how you should dress, to ensure you are not underdressing.

If you are highly uncertain about whether your dress is appropriate, call the human resources department and inquire about the appropriate interview dress—formal or casual. But if you have to choose between overdressing and underdressing, it is generally better to overdress. Underdressing sends the message "I am taking this interview casually; it is not very important to me." Overdressing might raise questions about whether you can fit into a more casual atmosphere, but those concerns can be offset with your demeanor and responses to questions. By overdressing, the message you will send is, "I care enough about securing this job that I made sure to dress in my finest attire as a sign of respect for you and for your firm."

Dressing Conservatively

Many career counselors will also tell you to dress "conservatively." By this, for men, they mean wear black or dark blue suits or slacks and white shirts. By this, for women, they generally mean you should not wear heavy makeup, heavy jewelry, bright colors, nail polish, perfume, or pants. (Only skirts or dresses are considered in some settings to be "conservative" attire for women.)

However, in today's business world, the rules are changing. Some women would be offended and would not want a job at a company that insisted that women should not wear pants to an interview. Some women therefore ignore that traditional rule and still fare well in the interviewing process. Likewise, some professionals like to dress in ways that celebrate their ethnic heritage, which might include brighter clothes or jewelry. The most cautious approach always is to dress conservatively, but many people choose to ignore some traditional advice in order to avoid any appearance of renouncing their own heritage or of kowtowing to a perceived old-boys' network that insists on skirts for women. If you choose to dress in bright designs or if you are a woman who chooses to wear pants to an interview, it is probably best to do so in a way that still allows you to appear well dressed. On the whole, many interviewers still frown on heavy makeup, heavy perfume, and nail polish.

Business Etiquette

Observing several basic etiquette rules also can help to create a great first impression. Here are some of the most important rules for interviews:

- **Arrive a few minutes early.** It is important that you not be late. It is also important that you are not too early—more than ten minutes before the appointment is too early and can be seen as rude or too aggressive. Arrive five to ten minutes early, as a sign that you are punctual and that this interview is important to you.

- **Arrive with a professional-looking pad and pen.** It is very important to some interviewers that you take some notes about what they say. Note-taking signifies that you find importance in what the interviewers are saying. However, do not take too many notes, and do not take notes if you believe jotting down a note will be interpreted as trying to bind the interviewer to some statement he or she might not want to be held to later. Use moderation, and before you start to take notes, ask the interviewer whether it is OK. Getting permission to take notes sets a good tone at the start of the interview.

- **Appear organized, carrying related documents with you.** For instance, if the employer supplied a list of all of the persons you should interview with, take the list with you on the day of your interviews. Also have a few copies of your résumé on hand in case any of the interviewers does not have your résumé readily available.

- **Shake hands with the interviewer.** When you meet the interviewer, be certain to shake hands with him or her. Keep your handshake firm and steady. You don't want a handshake that is too firm or too weak. A handshake that is limp is interpreted as weakness. One that is too hard is often construed as a sign of aggressiveness. A medium grip signifies confidence and warmth.

- **Wait to be asked to take a seat.** As a common etiquette practice, you should not move toward a seat and sit down until the interviewer points out where you should be seated and invites you to sit. If the interviewer does not do so right away, you can politely ask, "Where would you like me to sit?" This is a sign of respect.

- **Use the interviewer's last name.** You should treat the exchange as formal, using the interviewer's last name and proper title (Dr., Mrs., Ms., Mr.) unless the interviewer gives you permission to do otherwise. If you are not certain whether a woman's title is Mrs. or Miss, err on the side of caution by saying Ms. rather than asking for clarification.

How to Make a Good Impression in Informal Interviews: An Insider's View

Many candidates make the mistake of assuming that informal interviews do not influence an organization's ultimate decision about whether to extend a job offer. That assumption is often wrong. In any interaction, you are creating an impression. Therefore, what sorts of pitfalls should you avoid, and what are good impressions to try to make in an informal interview? They are much the same as in the formal interview. Here's what Edward, a manager at IBM, advises:

Common mistakes that candidates make in job interviews, informal and formal, include not preparing enough for the interview. Candidates should be ready with clear statements about their experiences, goals, and achievements. This begins with the first contact with a potential employer, and in formal *and* informal interviews, candidates should demonstrate they know plenty of details about the company and the available job. The résumé is also important. It should say something meaningful about a candidate's accomplishments and goals, and how those are related to the available job and the hiring company. The résumé should have integrity and be easy to read. The résumé should not have useless information that is not needed for the job the company is seeking to fill. It should not look like a cut-and-paste document constructed without reference to the specific job. In both formal and informal contacts with the interviewing company, the candidate should help the interviewer see how he or she fits with the available job and company, how the job and company fit with her or his goals, and what the value he or she can add.

Business Talk: Four Key Elements

In the earlier example of Jennifer on page 4, the bits of behavior that created a poor impression included her boisterous laughter, her questionable jokes, her poor dining etiquette, and her negative attitude. As we saw, when looking at Jennifer, one partner used a single question to guide his assessment about her: "Can I ever see myself wanting to introduce Jennifer to clients as a representative of our firm?" Observing her mannerisms, her demeanor, her attitude, and the topics of her conversation, he answered that question with a resounding, "No." There are some lessons to be learned here.

When interviewing—whether informally or formally—pay particular attention to four dimensions of what you do: your mannerisms, your etiquette, your attitude, and the topics you choose to discuss. Assume that you are being observed by those trying to envision whether they could ever put you in front of a client on an important deal. Thus, you should feel free to talk about noncontroversial current events, business events, uncontroversial company issues, industry trends, and topics such as sports. However, it is important that you stay away from important do-nots:

- Do not talk about controversial issues.
- Do not talk about issues that will make you seem overly negative.
- Do not crack risky jokes.
- Do not engage in boisterous talk.
- Do not overuse business jargon.
- Do not use slang unnecessarily.
- Try to avoid speaking negatively of your past employers (unless there is some important reason why you would want to do so).

Making the Most of Informational Interviews: An Insider's View

Many candidates wish to understand how top MBA candidates and other skilled interviewers are able to use informational or informal interviews to their advantage as tools for networking and introducing themselves to leaders in their field. Kelli Holden Hogan, founder and president of City Scholars Foundation, shares her insights. As a Harvard graduate who has worked for the leading companies Goldman Sachs and Pacific Bell, and who served as an executive recruiter for Los Angeles–based Berkhemer Clayton (where she assisted Harvard, Stanford, Berkeley, and Wharton MBAs with their career searches), Kelli notes key steps to ensure that you have an excellent informational interview:

Informational interviews—ones in which you meet professionals in order to gain information about their career path or their companies—

are key to career development. They offer a wonderful opportunity to meet senior-level executives with no strings attached. Most professionals find requests for informational interviews flattering. There are key ways to maximize this opportunity, and there are also many things to avoid.

Focus the conversation on the professional. First, if you secure an informational interview, make sure you focus the conversation on the professional who has agreed to meet with you, not on yourself. You should approach a professional for an informational interview by explaining that you are interested in speaking to him or her about their career and how he or she moved from their prior career positions to their current position, so as to get a better understanding of opportunities that might exist for you. Be sure to present your motives as pure. Avoid thrusting a résumé toward the informational interviewer early on or shifting the conversation to be about you and your own aspirations too soon. People love to talk about themselves, so by focusing the conversation on the professional and his or her career and achievements, you not only make the interviewer feel good, you also make a good impression.

Show respect: don't waste the interviewer's time. Even though this interaction is informal, it is crucial that you are respectful of the time of the professional who has agreed to meet with you. Never waste his or her time. When you approach the professional for the informational or informal interview, specify that you only wish to take about twenty minutes of his or her time. You can suggest you'd like to buy the interviewer a cup of coffee, so that he or she can share with you his or her experiences and how the individual made it to the current position. If he or she chooses to share more time, that's all the better.

Etiquette for the informational interview: dress the part, arrive early. To show respect, in an informal interview you must dress well— as well as you would for a formal interview. Similarly, just as you would for a formal interview, you need to arrive early for your meeting, but not too early to make the professional feel pressured to meet with you earlier. Ten or fifteen minutes early is ideal. Never take a chance that you will be late. That will leave the professional with the notion that you do not value his or her time, creating a negative, lasting impression.

Do your homework. Go to the informational interview well prepared. Just as with a formal interview, you should have researched the company and the professional with whom you are meeting by looking up company information on the corporate website and on the Internet, and by looking up the professional's bio on the Internet. Also conduct searches for any quotes or articles about the professional on the Internet. When you meet with your chosen professional, make it clear you are knowledgeable about his or her company and the professional's career. Do this by framing your questions appropriately. For instance, rather than asking a question such as "I understand you have been in your position for a year, how do you like it?" you might ask instead, "I understand you moved from the corporate development department to the finance department a year ago. How are you liking your new department?" The professional will be impressed that you have taken the time to read up both about him or her and about the company.

Take your résumé and a brief cover letter summarizing your experience. Finally, you should take with you a copy of your most recent résumé—one that has been tailored for the sort of position you say you are interested in pursuing—and a brief, bullet-point-style cover letter highlighting your achievements and skills. While you should focus most of your time on the professional and his or her experiences, it is fine to later transition the conversation to focus on you. At that time, you can present your résumé. Let the individual know you have been garnering relevant experiences and skills.

Close with style. As your meeting with the informational interviewer comes to a close, let the professional know that you have appreciated speaking at length with him or her, and that his or her perspectives have given you valuable insights. Reassure him or her how much you have learned; that will help to end the meeting on a very positive note. Finally, never forget to send a personal (oftentimes handwritten) thank-you note.

Dos and Don'ts of Informal and Formal Interviews: An Insider's View

Wilson Shelbon, who served as a manager at Procter & Gamble, explains what a world-class company looks for in a candidate:

I served as a manager at Procter & Gamble, where my responsibilities included leading teams of talented professionals, working long hours to analyze product costs and ways to reduce them, as well as working with teams to devise strategies that will make us more effective in the marketplace. When hiring, we selected candidates who we thought would do excellent work and blend well with us at Procter & Gamble. When I interviewed candidates from top schools, I used a number of factors to guide my decision making as to whether to support them in the hiring process. Several factors helped me think of some candidates as skilled interviewees—as candidates who interviewed like top MBAs—and as potentially excellent hires.

First, at Procter & Gamble, when we evaluated candidates, we took into great account key factors such as leadership abilities, analytical skills, problem-solving abilities, articulation, and creativity. You could not be perceived as too weak in any of these major areas and expect to get a job at a high level at Procter & Gamble. We especially valued candidates with extraordinary leadership abilities. We believed a manager who has potential to succeed in any functional areas and who will be tomorrow's business leader will possess outstanding leadership skills, because leaders drive change—every day managers at P&G are leading changes in the company as well as in the market. As managers, we devised strategies, analyzed market trends, performed competitive analysis, and so forth. So a candidate must create a lasting impression of his leadership abilities that wouldn't be erased during a formal interview.

So what is my advice to a candidate who is approaching both an informal and a formal interview? There are some don'ts. Don't go into any interview or interaction with a potential employer unprepared and lacking knowledge about the basics. You should have a sense of what the company does, and you should have read basic literature about the company. Don't be nervous! That creates a bad impression and will leave the interviewer questioning how he or she could put you in front of clients on team engagements. Don't fail to express yourself clearly. If you do, you will demonstrate a communication problem, and an interviewer will question whether you can contribute in teams and if you will be an asset in front of clients.

There are also dos. Do focus on the qualities such as leadership, initiative, and innovation that a winning candidate must have. This is a bit universal to all jobs, as these characteristics are all required in most business and managerial positions. Do provide examples when speaking about your qualifications. For example, it's hard to make the interviewer understand how strong your leadership is when you simply tell him that you are a great leader. Stories help illustrate. Let the facts speak for you! Be prepared to elaborate about your experiences that demonstrate your skills. We can tell how strong your skills and leadership are from your experiences.

Finally, in both an informal and a formal setting, try to demonstrate that you have a work ethic compatibility with the company and that you could blend into your potential new employer. Make sure your attitude toward teamwork or independent work fits with the job offered. Make sure to convey that your goals are compatible with those of the company. Those are among the most important things to get right.

Next Steps: Creating an Excellent Lasting Impression

Now that you know how to make a good first impression, the next step is to make an excellent *lasting* impression during an interview. The key to creating an outstanding lasting impression includes appearing prepared with knowledge and thoughtful responses about interview-relevant topics. To prepare, there are key steps to follow:

- **Do your homework.** Appear highly knowledgeable about four key interview-relevant areas: the industry, interviewing company, available job, and interviewer with whom you are meeting.

- **Know your résumé and be prepared to answer key questions effectively.** Be ready to discuss your résumé in depth. Be able to back up the claims on your résumé. And be prepared to respond to questions about your experience, work style, education, and goals.

The following nine chapters help you prepare to create a strong, lasting impression in your interview. They will elaborate on best practices for doing your homework before the interview and will explain how to use your résumé and your answers to key questions to deliver a winning interview.

CHAPTER 2

DO YOUR HOMEWORK IN FOUR KEY AREAS

Now that you have learned key elements about making a great first impression, it is important that you understand what some interviewers might expect of you in terms of preparation for a specific job interview. According to many Fortune 100 recruiters, headhunters, and career counselors, one of the most frequently cited mistakes candidates make in interviews is that they fail to come to the interview well informed in four critical interview-related areas. It is imperative that you learn the basics about the industry you hope to secure a job within, the company you are applying to work for, the available job you are applying for, and the person(s) who will be interviewing you.

Almost every Fortune 100 professional, headhunter, and career counselor with whom I spoke ranked this sort of interview preparedness very high. Given the importance of doing your homework and presenting yourself as knowledgeable, this chapter highlights key issues to consider about the industry, company, job, and people with whom you will be interviewing.

What to Know About Your Industry

One of the key topics you should research before you interview is the industry in which you want to work. The ideal depth of your industry knowledge will depend upon the level of job you are applying for. If you are interviewing for a position as a senior manager or executive, of course, you will be expected to know the industry intimately. Short of this, it is advisable that you have at least a basic understanding about the nature, dynamics, trends, and future direction of the industry. This information should help you in the interviewing process.

For instance, consider Lucas, who attended a job interview for a position as a general management consultant. He was asked, "How do you see yourself contributing to our firm, given the industry trends we are experiencing?"

Lucas found himself at a loss. He had been drawn to the strategic consulting job because the company was prestigious and the salary was large. He fumbled his way through his response, but the interviewer noted a marked lack of understanding of the issues affecting the industry and the trends affecting the company. Had Lucas taken the time to run a few searches online, using resources such as the *New York Times* or cnbc.com, he would have understood that the recession of 2002–2003 had severely hurt the consulting industry. Many consulting companies were shifting their focus to corporate restructuring work and were expanding their efforts to help distressed companies avoid bankruptcy. Lucas had skills that were germane to this restructuring work, but he was never able to talk about them, link them to industry trends, or elaborate on how he could use his background to help the interviewing company address its new work. A wonderful interviewing opportunity was lost as Lucas searched for a response.

So, what factors specifically are important? Keep things simple at first. If you need a great deal of in-depth information because you are applying for a high-level job, you can augment this base with more detailed information from specialized sources. To get started, focus on developing answers to three primary questions:

- What are the main characteristics of the industry? (Is it fast-paced, expanding, slowing, marked by innovation, marked by intense competition by a few giant competitors?)
- What challenges or trends are currently affecting the industry?
- Where is the industry heading in the long term?

Table 2.1 Key Areas of Information About the Industry

Basic Understanding of the Industry	Sample Questions This Knowledge Will Help You Answer
What are the main characteristics of this industry?	Why is this the right industry for you? What factors make this industry appealing to you?
What challenges or trends currently affect the industry?	How can you use your skills to help the company meet the industry challenges it faces?
Where is the industry heading in the long term?	Where do you see yourself in five years, given the changes and direction of the industry?

Gaining that broad understanding will be useful as you proceed through the interviewing process. Table 2.1 suggests how your understanding of the industry can help you address interview questions.

Resources to Consider

When researching the industry in which you hope to work, useful sources include the following:

News Media. You can conduct searches about the industry using local newspapers or national newspapers and magazines such as the *New York Times*, the *Wall Street Journal*, the *Washington Post*, *Business Week*, and *Fortune* magazine. You can also conduct online research using archived articles at network TV news websites, such as ABC News (abcnews .com), CNN (cnn.com), and CNBC (cnbc.com).

Search Engines. Search engines such as Google (google.com), Yahoo (yahoo.com), and Hotbot (hotbot.com) can lead you to articles and other references about your industry.

Online Companies. For more detailed information about industries, several sources provide useful overviews. Consider Vault.com, Monster .com, and Tractiva.

Standard & Poor's Reports. For good industry overviews, secure Standard & Poor's (S&P) industry reports. Take a look at their resources at standardpoors.com.

What to Learn About the Industry Before Interviewing: An Insider's View

How important is the depth of your knowledge about an industry during an interview? Is it necessary to garner information about the industry, rather than just about the company? Knowledge about an industry can be very important. Some employers will ask you to explain in detail why a particular industry or career—not just a particular company—is right for you, given your personality and experience. Susan Kim, the head of the successful advisory group Kim, Hopkins & Associates—one of the largest franchises of American Express Financial Advisors in the Washington, D.C., area, with approximately $35 million under management—explains how you can use information about an industry to interview like a top MBA:

In providing advice on how to use information about an industry in ways that help you to deliver an outstanding interview, I draw on my own experience at the Fortune 100 company American Express. Several approaches have worked for me and have also impressed me as I have interviewed and hired job candidates.

What information should you gather about an industry? First, gain an understanding of the overall structure of the industry to which you are applying. In the case of American Express Financial Advisors, you should know the industry of financial planning and how it differs from related industries such as investment banking. Within financial planning, you should have an understanding of who the main players are. Know which companies dominate the arena and how they differ from each other. Also answer for yourself key questions, such as, "How many independent planners are out there, and what role do they play in the industry?"

When I was seeking employment in financial planning, gaining an understanding of these factors was very important. When I first made my transition to the financial planning arena, I noted that only a small percentage of professionals in the field were planners; most other professionals were brokers. I could see that there was a tremendous growth opportunity in the financial planning industry and that someone with compatible goals and initiative could build a flourishing career. After I gained this understanding about the structure and characteristics of the industry, I took that information and related it in my interviews to why I was choosing this industry, and how my personal characteristics made me ideal for this particular profession. You must do the same thing in order to interview like a top MBA.

In my case, I was a mathematics and economics major in college, and then I taught math for a number of years. When I was ready to make the transition to become a financial adviser, I had to communicate to American Express why my background and my personal characteristics made me excellent for financial planning. My ability to clearly express these points was critical to my success.

For instance, my math and economics background meant that I had developed excellent analytical skills, as well as a deep understanding of the microeconomic and macroeconomic issues that all leading financial advisers must master. I was able to communicate how my background in math and economics, as well as my internships, had given me skills relevant to the financial advising sector. I also conveyed how my passion for numbers was also ideal in this industry.

Similarly, my experience as a mathematics teacher came in handy. I was able to articulate how I am a people person, how I love working with clients, and how I am excellent at teaching, building trust, and maintaining the confidence of those with whom I work. My time as a teacher also meant I was good at guiding others to make sound decisions. These characteristics became assets because I had the opportunity to clearly explain why the financial advising industry was perfect for me.

Finally, as the mother of two small children, I was seeking a career that provided flexibility with time. Through the autonomy I would gain as I became a successful financial adviser with a large client base, I could see that the financial planning industry could give me that flexibility.

During my interviews, when I was seeking a job as a financial planner with American Express, I articulated these key points well. I impressed my future employers because my personal characteristics and my goals were ideally suited to and compatible with the characteristics of the industry to which I was applying. As a result, I successfully landed the job I was seeking.

What to Know About the Company Interviewing You

You should also become highly literate about the company where you will be interviewing. This is clearly important, as you want to demonstrate to the interviewer that you are serious about wanting the position. To appear serious about this, you need to have considered deeply whether the company is the right one for you. To articulate reasons, you should be able to point out its distinguishing characteristics that attract you and then state why the interviewing company is a better choice for you than its main competitors.

What factors specifically are important? Start with these key areas of understanding:

- The company's main products or services
- The main competitors of the company
- What makes the company unique
- The company's mission
- The company's profitability and growth
- The corporate culture of the company
- The company's strategy (for example, whether it is repositioning itself or expanding its products and services in any notable way)

This broad understanding will be useful to you as you proceed through the interviewing process. In particular, knowing this information can help you respond to common interview questions. See Table 2.2.

Table 2.2 What to Know About the Company You Are Interviewing With

Basic Understanding of the Company	Sample Questions This Knowledge Will Help You Answer
What are the company's main products and services?	What interests you most about this company?
Who are the company's main competitors?	Why would you choose our company over our competitors?
What makes the company unique?	Why do you believe this is the best company for you?
What is the company's mission?	How do your values fit with our mission?
How has the company been faring in terms of profitability or growth?	How do you believe you can help this company become more profitable?
What is the corporate culture of the company?	Do you believe you will fit into this office?
Is the company repositioning itself or expanding its products and services in any notable way?	Where do you see yourself in two years?

Mistakes to Avoid When Speaking About the Company: An Insider's View

Here's what Tats, a manager at Tokio Marine Group, advises the successful candidate not to do:

One thing that really makes for a poor interview, in my opinion, is when a candidate clearly did not make any effort to do research about the company and cannot state his or her reason for selecting our company rather than our competitors. That does not assure us that the candidate believes this will be a fit. It also does not assure us that the candidate would take an offer from us seriously, or that he or she wants the job enough. Another thing to avoid when interviewing is speaking about the company in terms of its stability and high salary; those reasons alone should not be reason for selecting a firm. A candidate should clearly express why our firm is right for them, demonstrate knowledge about our firm, and then tie that information to notions about their uniqueness compared with other candidates. Namely, they should answer the question for us of "Why him/her and not the next candidate waiting in line?"

Resources to Consider

When you are researching the company with which you hope to interview, the following sorts of sources are useful:

Company Website. One of the first information sources you should review is the website of the company you are applying to. You can surf the company's website to discover the mission statement, structure, size, locations, and areas of specialization. Also, many sites post news releases; these might reveal information about the company's plans.

Newspapers and Magazines. You can complete searches of local newspapers and national newspapers and magazines such as the *New York Times*, *Wall Street Journal*, *Washington Post*, *Business Week*, *Money* magazine, *Kiplinger*, and *Fortune*. You can also conduct online research to find archived articles at network-TV news websites, such as ABC News, NBC News, CBS News, CNBC, and CNN.

Specialized News Resources. For candidates wishing to gain perspectives of companies from the vantage points of minorities or women, sources such as *Black Enterprise*, *Ebony* magazine, and *Essence* magazine can provide useful perspectives and often provide rankings of good companies to work for.

Search Engines. Search engines such as Google, Yahoo, and Hotbot can lead you to articles and other references about your company.

Specialized and Sophisticated Sources. For more detailed and sophisticated information about companies, several sources provide in-depth information about companies. Try Hoover's Online, Bloomberg .com, Vault.com, and Tractiva.

Annual Reports and SEC Filings. Annual reports and public filings with the Securities and Exchange Commission also provide detailed information for candidates who believe they will be expected to be intimately familiar with the interviewing company.

Formal and Informal Personal Networks. Contact your friends, acquaintances, or former schoolmates who work for the company or who might have knowledge about the company. Speak with them to gain an inside or more detailed perspective on the company. Alumni or professional organizations are particularly useful.

Job Fairs. Job fairs, in which companies make presentations and provide company information, are also useful for understanding key facts about a company.

Headhunters. Executive career placement professionals are usually very literate about companies in their fields of specialization and the distinguishing characteristics among companies.

What to Learn About the Company Before You Interview: An Insider's View

Many job candidates want to know what top MBAs and other skilled interviewees have learned about how to appear prepared excellently for an interview. One key step is to ensure the interviewer realizes you are interested in the job enough to have done your homework about the company. What specific information should you know? Celeste Garcia, a Harvard graduate who became a senior-level consultant with PricewaterhouseCoopers and now serves as managing director of consulting services for the D.C.-based Ivy Planning Group, LLC, shares the best practices she has learned through her successful career. She also provides insights into what impresses her as she interviews top MBAs for jobs today:

There are critical sorts of information that any serious candidate should know when walking through the door of an interview. This includes all knowledge about the company that can be garnered from the corporate website. It will be assumed that you have at least read that, and it will make a bad impression if you have not. You should also have a firm understanding of the company's products and services, its customers, and its overall direction. For instance, if the company is a consulting company, are the main clients federal entities, state agencies, or Fortune 500 companies? Is it based more solidly in the private or the public sector? In the practice area that you hope to join within the company, who are the main competitors? What types of professionals does the company recruit? What is the employment structure within the career path? Where does the company operate? How long has the company been in operation, and how have its products or services changed in recent years?

It is always bothersome to meet an interviewee who asks basic questions that are answered on our website. Without demonstrating that you have a solid understanding of the company, you will likely leave the interviewer with the impression that you are not serious about the job, that you would really prefer to work elsewhere and are comparison shopping. Given how crucial preparation is to having an excellent interview, let me explain how to secure the appropriate information and what to do once you have it.

Securing the Information. After reading the corporate website, you should conduct a general search on the Internet for recent press about the company (good and bad, for the past few years). Also secure basic information about the company's main competitors, products, and services. Beyond doing Internet research using the corporate website and reviewing press about the company, there are some sources of informal information that you might consider tapping into. For instance, use your college or high school alumni networks to speak with alumni who might be working for the company you hope to interview with. They may be willing to speak with you outside of the formal interviewing process. Use information from these contacts to get an inside story about the company, its competitors, its services and goods, and how the company differs from its competitors. Perhaps even have a friend or fellow alumni introduce you to the relevant personnel within the company.

How to Best Use Information About the Company. Form is important. Don't inundate an interviewer with too many facts that they already know. Someone can know a whole lot and come across as too pushy or still ask silly questions; that person will create a negative impression. Instead, subtly and skillfully weave in references, so it is clear to the interviewer that you have researched the company well. For instance, rather than asking, "Tell me about your consulting practice," you might ask, "I know your company takes a quantitative approach to process improvement, so I would be interested to know what sorts of process improvement projects you foresee in the future." If given the chance to ask questions at the end of the interview, take the opportunity to make references to what you have read, and ask questions that are valued-added. Rather than "Do you have a change management practice?" the question should be, "I read on your website that you have a growing integration management practice. How do you weave integration management into your various practices?"

What to Know About the Specific Job Offered

Before interviewing, you should also become as familiar as possible with the job you are applying for and its associated roles and responsibilities. You should seek out a formal job description from the human resources department or another reliable source, and you should seek an understanding of these aspects of the position:

- What are the educational requirements and work experience requirements for the position?
- How many people will you be managing, if any?
- What will your primary tasks and functions be?
- To whom will you report?
- Will you be working in teams or individually?
- Are special technical or writing skills required?

Gaining this broad understanding will be useful to you as you proceed through the interview process. In particular, knowing this information can help you respond to the questions in Table 2.3.

Table 2.3 Questions to Ask About the Specific Job

Basic Understanding of the Position for Which You Are Applying	Sample Questions This Knowledge Will Help You Answer
What are the educational requirements?	How is your educational background relevant to this position?
What are the work experience requirements?	How has your work experience prepared you for this position?
How many people will you be managing, if any?	Tell me about your managerial experience.
What will be your primary tasks and functions?	What makes you feel qualified to complete the primary tasks of this job?
To whom will you report?	How do you interact best with your superiors?
Will you be working in teams or individually?	What factors do you believe help create good teamwork?
Are special technical or writing skills required?	Tell me about any special skills you have that you believe can enhance your performance in this job.

Resources to Consider

When attempting to locate a good job description for the position you are applying for, you might request that the interviewing organization's human resources department send you a precise job description. Other reliable sources include official job postings that the company has sent out.

What to Know About the Job Before You Interview: An Insider's View

A skilled interviewee should go into an interview with a solid understanding of the position he or she is seeking. What helps a candidate come across as extremely well prepared? Fred Clayton, former head of the Price Waterhouse western U.S. executive search practice and partner at Ward Howell International and now president and CEO of the Los Angeles–based executive search firm Berkhemer Clayton, Inc., offers his insight:

During my twenty-three years of work as an executive recruiter, I have presented top executives with MBAs from Stanford, Berkeley, and Harvard. Of the key skills these excellent interviewees showed during the interviewing process, most important was the knowledge that the interviewing candidate demonstrated about the position for which they were applying. Several things, done well, will leave the interviewer with the impression that you interview like a top MBA and you will likely be a great fit for their position. Here are some steps I recommend.

First, review the position description well before the interview. You usually have access to a short version through a job posting, but see if there is a longer version available, either by calling the human resources contact or looking for more information on the company website. If the job search is not confidential, you can also take the opportunity to network, asking friends or sources in that company for extra background about the potential job. You can also approach friends or colleagues who hold similar positions in other companies in that industry to help you. Understanding the type of position, the job responsibilities, and what the job will be like in the crucial first year that you walk through the door will help you guide the interviewer to discuss your relevant experience and skills.

Second, find out whether the position is new or a replacement position. This is important, particularly at higher levels of the organization. If the position is new, your role may principally be defined as builder—building new management processes, building new teams, building new clientele. If instead you will be replacing someone, particularly at a high level of an organization, then your role may be principally to lead a turn-around situation, fixing problems that might exist in the department.

By knowing whether your role will be "replacement-turnaround" or "new-builder," you will be able to reflect on your experience better and prepare more appropriate responses to questions. This is particularly important when you encounter "behavioral" questions from skilled interviewers who ask questions such as "Give me an example of how you have handled this sort of situation." You can better anticipate which situations the interviewer is more likely to ask you about.

Third, remember, it is up to you to relate your experience to the position offered. You will likely have two or three interviews at a company, and perhaps more, before you reach the offer stage. The inter-viewers may be skillful or relatively inexperienced. And the "ultimate" interviewer, the person to whom you would report if hired, may be an excellent manager but not very skilled as an interviewer. If you are not asked questions that you think would bring out important information about your background, you must find a way to weave that information into your conversation.

On this point, a very important piece of advice is to get the inter-viewer to do the talking as soon as you sit down with them. Ask the interviewer to describe the job responsibilities in greater depth. This gives you, the interviewee, the opportunity to understand how you should be looking at the job and how to deliver the right message about your relevant skills and experience. This is much better than starting to describe your achievements and your background without a better understanding of the job.

What to Know About the Professional Interviewing You

Finally, you should do your homework about the person interviewing you. Normally, this need not take much time or effort. You can simply surf the company's website and pull the biography of the person who will be interviewing you, if that bio is available. If a biography is not available, it might be worthwhile to put in a call to human resources simply to determine the interviewer's title and position in the firm, so you are clear about whom you will be meeting with.

Sometimes, knowing the biography of the person who will be inter-viewing you can help you determine which topics you can chat about to help develop a good personal rapport. For instance, if you discover that your interviewer attended your college, you know before the interview that you can speak at length about the interviewer's college days in order to strike up a more personal dialogue. Likewise, if you discover that you and your interviewer are from the same hometown, you will immedi-ately have a large number of topics that you can broach in order to estab-lish a friendly dialogue with the interviewer during your discussion.

If you consider it necessary, you can also conduct more extensive searches using resources such as Google and newspapers online to find information about the professionals who will be interviewing you for a job. For the most part, only very prominent company professionals will be mentioned in articles searchable with Internet search engines or online newspapers.

Knowing About the Interviewer and Personalizing an Interview: An Insider's View

What sorts of information should you try to gather about the person who will be interviewing you? How can you best collect that information? Byron, a Harvard graduate with experience at the top firms McKinsey & Company and Booz Allen Hamilton, uses his experience as a successful hire and his interaction with graduates from MBA and law programs such as those at Harvard, Stanford, and Yale to provide insights about best practices to employ in order to interview like a top MBA:

In my view, the most important information to gather prior to an interview is information about the industry, the company, and the specific job. The main thing the interviewer is looking for is someone who can perform well on the job. It is an important additional touch if you are able to also gather information about the interviewer. That information can help you deliver responses that are more tailored to the specific person who will influence the hiring decision.

What sorts of information should you look for about the interviewer? Educational background is always relevant. If you attended the same school, that would be a great way to personalize your conversation with the interviewer. If you went to school in the same region of the country, that too can serve as a basis for personalizing your comments in the interview. Other sorts of information you should be looking for include the interviewer's project background. Know what sorts of work the interviewer has done or gravitates toward; this information can help you avoid missteps in your comments to the interviewer. Personal background, such as where the interviewer grew up or what their hobbies are, can also help you make references that add a nice personal touch.

Here are some steps that have brought me, as well as top law school graduates and MBAs whom I have worked with, success in the interviewing process:

Gather written information about the interviewer's background. You should search the company website and the Internet for information about your interviewer. The more senior the interviewer is in the company, the more information you are likely to find. How will you use this information? You can add a personal touch to the interview by making reference, for instance, to the interviewer's educational background. This can provide good conversation points during an interview. Generally, interviewers are impressed if you appear to have bothered to gain information about their backgrounds or their careers.

Leverage contacts. Leverage your friends and acquaintances to gain information about the interviewer. This can include brief discussions to find out what your friends know of the interviewer, if they know him or her directly. It can also include access to other information, such as a bio or résumé about the interviewer to which a friend or acquaintance may have access.

Ask the interviewer. Despite your best efforts, you may find it difficult to locate information about the interviewer. So don't be bashful about asking the interviewer directly in the interview. It can be a great practice to be straightforward and ask about the interviewer's background and how their job fits into their overall goals and ambitions. People like nothing better than to talk about themselves. Leverage this tendency.

For example, in my interviews, which enabled me to land a job with one of the top consulting companies in the world, I laid the groundwork for the interviewer to talk after first demonstrating that I knew a great deal about the industry and the available job. I had learned as much as possible about the industry and the job. I had done my research and was able to speak using industry terms such as *section 508* and *GPEA*, to sound like someone who had worked in the government consulting industry area before. After making those solid impressions, I prompted the interviewer to talk about his own background. This enabled me to take the interview to a whole new level. I established a strong rapport with the interviewer, and I left an excellent impression. In fact, part of my success in the interviewing process can be in part attributed to how, in many cases, I have succeeded in getting interviewers to talk about themselves for half of the interview! My interviewers always end our conversations saying they were great.

Another example of how an interview can be personalized is when you are able to pick up on "sidebar" comments, such as when the interviewer mentions children (indicating a strong value toward family life), sports teams (strong values of life outside of work), etc. A skilled interviewee, one who interviews like a top MBA, will actively look for such references and leverage them to his or her advantage during the interview.

By gathering information about an interviewer's professional, educational, and personal background, you will be able to speak about subjects other than professional topics during the interview and create a good connection with the interviewer. This information can also help you avoid mistakes. If you are aware that the interviewer went to a rival school and is very sensitive about your education at their school's rival—information that you could have discovered through friends—that information can help you to speak carefully about your school. Never give the interviewer an opportunity to dislike you for subjective reasons. Similarly, if you were to ask an interviewer about their background during the interview, you should be an excellent listener and take opportunities to elaborate on things about which the interviewer feels passionately, and avoid topics that seem sensitive.

Now that you know about best practices and what sorts of information you should review to deepen your knowledge before the interview, you should be able to become much more informed about the relevant industry, company, job, and interviewer before attending your job interview. Use this knowledge to refine your responses and to interview like a top MBA.

CHAPTER 3

USE YOUR RÉSUMÉ AS AN EFFECTIVE INTERVIEWING TOOL

Another important step to performing excellently in a job interview is making effective use of your résumé as a tool in the interviewing process. Headhunters, career counselors, and Fortune 100 recruiters agree that failure to use a résumé effectively is one of the top reasons why candidates fare poorly in interviews. Here are two tips for using your résumé effectively. First, you must use the résumé to present a powerful and tailored portrait of your job-relevant skills and experiences, woven together strategically with strong indications of a coherent story line, indicating the broader purpose behind your educational and career choices. Your résumé should be carefully crafted to show a match between your qualifications and those of the ideal candidate for the job. Second, you must be able to back up your claims on your résumé and be able to respond to questions in depth, further demonstrating that your qualifications and experiences fit the requirements of your desired job. This chapter focuses on the first of these requirements—tailoring your résumé to demonstrate a fit. Chapter 4 will describe how to back up the information on your résumé and respond to queries in depth.

Using Your Résumé to Demonstrate a Match

One of the first principles you should embrace when trying to use your résumé as an effective tool in the interviewing process is to make sure you tailor your résumé as needed to each job for which you are applying. You are seeking to create the notion that your qualifications and experiences match what the interviewer believes are those of the ideal job candidate. To be called for an interview, you have to create in the interviewer's mind a belief that there is the possibility for such a fit. Here are six key steps to help tailor your résumé for a specific job opportunity:

1. **Create the interviewer's checklist.** Use the job description and your understanding of the available position to assess the job requirements and profile of an ideal candidate.
2. **Assess your record in three dimensions.** These are work experience, education, and extracurricular activities.
3. **Highlight relevant experience.** Use the interviewer's checklist to prune your résumé.
4. **Prioritize.** Use the interviewer's checklist to strategically structure your content.
5. **Phrase effectively.** Phrasing matters! Use action words, "fit phrases" (that demonstrate a match between your qualifications and those of the ideal candidate), and "leadership language" to describe your experience.
6. **Final check.** Complete a final check to avoid common résumé mistakes.

Create the Interviewer's Checklist

A first useful exercise in tailoring your résumé for a specific job is to assess the job's requirements and try to consider what the ideal candidate for that job might look like in the eyes of the interviewer. In this way, you are creating the interviewer's checklist. In fact, many companies employ a very systematic recruiting process providing interviewers grids or checklists with which they rate candidates. In some companies, if you are not rated high in most categories on their checklist, you might not be considered a serious candidate. In completing this exercise of creating the interviewer's checklist, you are compiling a hypothetical checklist that you can use to discern areas of weakness in your application. It will also help you pinpoint your strengths, experience, skills, and knowledge that you should emphasize on your résumé.

The Sample Job Assessment Work Sheet provides an example of this process. It maps out the core responsibilities, tasks, and skills associated with a particular job and helps to highlight the most desirable attributes that an ideal job candidate might possess.

SAMPLE JOB ASSESSMENT WORK SHEET

Sample Formal Job Description

The Omni Consulting Group is seeking an MBA-level professional for its position as an associate. The associate will join a team of professionals, providing strategic and organizational design advice to leading companies in the high-technology sector. The associate will report directly to the vice president, manage three junior associates, and will interact frequently with key clients.

Sample Assessment of Job Requirements

Using the formal job description, I have completed Part A of the work sheet, mapping out the main responsibilities, tasks, and skills needed for this position. When formulating your list of associated tasks, I tried to envision the work an associate might be required to complete on a daily or weekly basis.

Part A

Top Five Responsibilities

Provide strategic advice to high-technology companies
Provide organizational design advice to high-technology companies
Manage teamwork of Junior Associates
Facilitate work between team and client
Serve as support for Vice President's work

Associated Tasks

Oversee research and compilation of data about challenges faced by high-technology clients

Stay abreast of trends affecting the high-technology sector
Set team goals, assign team tasks, review work products of team members
Mentor junior team members
Meet with Vice President to keep him/her abreast of team activities and progress
Meet with client to ensure client's needs are met and to address client's concerns
Meet with client to coordinate collection of data or to present findings

Associated Skills/Knowledge

Research skills
Familiarity with data resources
Familiarity with high-technology concerns
Analytical skills
Team participation skills
Team leadership skills
Time management skills
Client management skills
Presentation skills

Sample Profiling the Ideal Candidate

Given the assessment of the job responsibilities, tasks, and associated skills, I have completed Part B of the work sheet, mapping out the ideal work experience, education, skills/knowledge, personal attributes, and goals that an ideal candidate might possess.

Part B

Ideal Work Experience

Experience managing teams
Experience participating in teams
Experience coaching team members
Client management experience
Experience collecting, sifting through, and assessing of data
Experience formulating recommendations
Experience making presentations to clients
Experience working as liaison between upper management and teams

Ideal Education

MBA degree, undergraduate degree in sciences or engineering (major relevant to high technology)
Education that included courses requiring collection and analysis of data
Education that included participation in team projects

Ideal Skills/Knowledge

Research skills
Analytical skills
Familiarity with data resources and high-technology concerns
Team participation skills
Team leadership skills
Time management skills
Client management skills
Presentation skills

Ideal Personal Attributes

Organized
Motivated
Good communicator
Good problem solver
Goal oriented
Innovative
Cooperative
Good team player/leader

Ideal Short- or Long-Term Career Goals

Short-term: Desire to help high-technology companies perform excellently and continue to innovate

Long-term: No particular requirement but perhaps a desire to help lead the interviewing company's high-technology practice

Assess Three Dimensions of Your Record: Work Experience, Education, Extracurricular or Outside-of-Work Activities

Now that you have seen an example, take the opportunity to assess the job descriptions for jobs you hope to secure. Construct a profile of the ideal candidate for each job. After you have mapped out your potential employer's checklist of an ideal candidate's qualities, it will be time for you to assess your own strengths and weaknesses. You will prepare to craft your résumé in a way that helps portray you as a match for the position.

JOB ASSESSMENT WORK SHEET

Formal Job Description

_____

_____

_____

Assessment of Job Requirements

Using the formal job description, map out the main responsibilities, tasks, and skills needed in this position.

Top Five Responsibilities

_____

_____

_____

Associated Tasks

_____

_____

_____

Associated Skills/Knowledge

_____

_____

_____

Profiling the Ideal Candidate

Given your assessment of the job requirements, map out the ideal work experience, education, skills/knowledge, personal attributes, and career goals that an ideal candidate would possess.

Ideal Work Experience

_____

_____

_____

Ideal Education

_____

_____

_____

Ideal Skills/Knowledge

_____

_____

_____

Ideal Personal Attributes

_____

_____

_____

Ideal Short- or Long-Term Career Goals

_____

_____

_____

You will use your assessment to help determine what to emphasize on the résumé you tailor for this job.

Now that you have constructed a profile of an ideal candidate, you should examine your work experience, education, and extracurricular activities to pinpoint the aspects of your record that you want to highlight to promote yourself as qualified for the job.

Work Experience

Using your analysis in the Job Assessment Work Sheet on pages 38–39, complete an analysis about the ways in which each of the jobs you have held, either full-time or part-time, has helped you to demonstrate relevant experience, skills, or knowledge.

Assessment of Your Recent Jobs

On the Professional Record Work Sheet, map out the main responsibilities, tasks, and skills associated with your most recent position. In the top portion of the same work sheet, list the responsibilities, associated tasks, and associated skills that are most relevant to the job for which you will apply. List all other responsibilities, tasks, and skills of your most recent full-time job in the lower portion of the work sheet.

PROFESSIONAL RECORD WORK SHEET: MOST RECENT JOB

Aspects to emphasize on your tailored résumé.

Most Relevant Responsibilities

_____

_____

_____

_____

Most Relevant Associated Tasks

_____

_____

_____

Most Relevant Associated Skills _____

_____

_____

Other Responsibilities _____

_____

_____

_____

Associated Tasks _____

_____

_____

_____

Associated Skills _____

_____

_____

_____

On your résumé, you should try to emphasize the responsibilities, tasks, skills, and knowledge that are most relevant to your desired new job. Elaborate about those at greater length than the responsibilities in the bottom half of the work sheet, which are less relevant to the job you seek to secure.

You can use this same work sheet to assess jobs you held before your most recent job. Additional work sheets can be found in the Appendix.

Use these assessments to decide what information to highlight on your résumé.

Educational Record

Similarly, you should attempt to discern the key ways in which your education can be seen as relevant to the job you hope to secure. Use the Educational Record Work Sheet that follows to help you pinpoint knowledge, skills, or courses that make you more qualified for the job you are seeking. List the courses that are directly relevant to the job you are seeking and list any associated knowledge or skills. For instance, if you are applying for a job as a marketing specialist, you might high-

---

EDUCATIONAL RECORD WORK SHEET

Education Information (Name of Institution, Degree): _____

_____

Relevant Courses

_____

_____

_____

Associated Certificates/Training/Knowledge

_____

_____

_____

Associated Skills

_____

_____

_____

---

light a marketing course such as Advanced Marketing Techniques that you completed in college. In that case, you could list as associated knowledge information such as "techniques to determine ideal distribution channels," or "techniques for communicating value of products." Associated skills could include "ability to use pricing methodology," or "ability to assess marketing data."

Extracurricular or Outside-of-Work Activities Record

Finally, determine the key ways in which your extracurricular or outside-of-work activities can be seen as relevant to the job you hope to secure. Using your Job Assessment Work Sheet as a guide, complete an analysis of the ways in which each of the main extracurricular activities you have participated in has helped you demonstrate relevant experience, skills, or knowledge.

Assessment of a Main Extracurricular or Outside-of-Work Activities

Map out the main responsibilities, tasks, and skills associated with each of your significant extracurricular or outside-of-work activities, using the Extracurricular Record Work Sheet. In the top half of the work sheet, list the activities that are relevant to the responsibilities, associated tasks, or associated skills of the job you hope to secure. On your résumé, you might add one description line beneath your extracurricular or outside-of-work listings to describe and highlight the way it adds to your qualifications for the available job. (Please note, it is not uncommon for you to find that some of your extracurricular activities are not very relevant to your job search.)

Fill in the following extracurricular/outside-of-work activities work sheet to determine whether some of your extracurricular activities help demonstrate your qualifications for the job you desire. If they do, consider highlighting those activities in your interview and/or on your résumé. Refer to the filled-in sample work sheet for guidance.

SAMPLE EXTRACURRICULAR RECORD WORK SHEET

In the following sample, Pat, an applicant for a position as a manager at a retail bookstore, has analyzed her specific outside-of-work activity:

Extracurricular or Outside-of-Work Activity

Executive Board Member, Chicago Women's Business Association (Chicago, IL)

Relevant Responsibilities

Play integral role on committee of ten in leading this club of more than 1,000 professionals in the Chicago area. Oversee the direction of club to subsequently help steer direction, ensuring that the needs of members are met.

Relevant Tasks

Help set strategy for organization. Design campaigns to increase membership and gain feedback on desires of members. Lead committees to plan desired activities. Help implement programs. Organize professional seminars.

Relevant Skills/Knowledge

Setting organizational strategy. Leading teams. Organizing learning seminars. Implementing programs. Analyzing and responding to feedback.

Relevant Personal Attributes Demonstrated

Leadership, initiative, teamwork, dedication to hard work, commitment to community, detail orientation

* Note, the "relevant" responsibilities, tasks, knowledge/skills, and personal attributes are those that help demonstrate that you have experience, knowledge/skills, and personal qualities that will make you qualified for the particular job for which you are interviewing.

EXTRACURRICULAR/OUTSIDE-OF-WORK ACTIVITIES WORK SHEET

Extracurricular or Outside-of-Work Activity

_____

_____

_____

Relevant Responsibilities

_____

_____

_____

Relevant Tasks

_____

_____

_____

Relevant Skills/Knowledge

_____

_____

_____

Relevant Personal Attributes Demonstrated

_____

_____

_____

When you have completed an assessment and are aware of what aspects of your work experience, education, and extracurricular or outside-of-work activities help you demonstrate a fit for your desired job, your next task is to organize this information into a résumé. Use the following general principles to help compile a strategically designed résumé.

Common Résumé Mistakes: An Insider's View

Verizon Telecommunication's Malli had this to say about the finer points of a résumé:

One problem I have seen in résumés is the failure to place educational information in the ideal place on the résumé. If you have been out of school for several years, put your education qualifications last or at the bottom of the page. I know of a case in which a candidate displayed his Ph.D. very prominently on page 1, even though he had twenty years of post-Ph.D. work experience. That told me that this candidate did not likely have any significant real-world experiences that would be useful to us.

One thing to do well on the résumé: try to highlight "soft" skills that can serve as the common denominators in both a nontraditional and a mainstream job.

Prioritize and Prune: Highlight Relevant Experience

To structure your résumé, you can use your assessment of your own work experience, education, and extracurricular activities to decide which parts of your record should receive the most attention on the résumé. Elaborate at greatest length about the activities that help you convey relevant experience, skills, and knowledge.

Prioritize your résumé by relegating irrelevant work experience to a category lower on the résumé, in a section that you might label "Other Work Experience." Keep the central part of the résumé focused on relevant experience. Similarly, you should prune your résumé, giving more space to work experience that the interviewer is likely to value. Do not elaborate at length about your education, except to indicate awards, distinctions, and information that highlight relevant knowledge and skills.

The key to carving your résumé for a specific job is just that: you are carving it, drawing attention to the aspects of your education and professional experience that demonstrate you have been picking up relevant skills and experiences over the years. Consider the instance of Elaine, who completed four summer internships: two in law firms, one in a government agency, and a fourth in an artist's studio. Elaine decides upon graduation that she will apply for a job as a paralegal at a law firm. To carve her résumé well, she gave greater prominence to her two law firm internships and her government agency position. She placed information about her internship at the artist's studio in a category lower on the résumé called "other experience." While she still includes information about the artist's studio internship to reveal all of her work experience, she skillfully uses the résumé in a way that calls the most attention to experiences that relate to the job she is applying for—a paralegal position. When she enters the job interview, therefore, the interviewer will focus on the experiences that are most relevant and that convey the skills that will help Elaine excel as a paralegal.

You should also prioritize the details you provide when describing your work experience, education, and extracurricular activities. Prioritize the description details of your résumé by placing any details, wherever possible, with the most relevant information first. The information least relevant to the job you are applying for should go last. In doing so, you can help create an initial impression of a match—one you will hope to sustain and deepen during your interview.

Résumé Mistakes to Avoid: An Insider's View

Isabell, of Staples, Inc., describes the differences among duties, skills, and accomplishments:

Common mistakes I see in résumés for candidates applying for jobs include instances where a candidate is too focused on job duties rather than skills and accomplishments. Another mistake occurs when a candidate presents a general and vague objective statement that adds little to the résumé, or fails to utilize action verbs in the job descriptions. That is not ideal, because we want to know about the skills and accomplishments. Similarly, for mainstream jobs a candidate should usually emphasize business skills rather than technical proficiency on a résumé and during the interview.

Describe Work Experience Effectively—
Phrasing Matters

Phrasings matter a great deal on résumés as well as in the interview itself. Make an effort to convey through your résumé language an image that is goal oriented and proactive. You can do this through use of *action verbs* or *leadership language*. For instance, rather than saying you participated in a team, you might say you "helped *lead* a team" (leadership language). Instead of saying your responsibilities included meeting with a client, you could indicate that you "*nurtured* client relationships" (using an action verb). Make sure that when you employ this type of leadership language, however, that you are not exaggerating your responsibilities.

You should sprinkle your résumé with fit phrases, but do not do this too extensively. *Fit phrases* are ones that weave in the language associated with the profile of the ideal candidate for the available job. For example, in our Sample Job Assessment Work Sheet on page 35–37, we determined that an ideal candidate for the associate position would have experience advising clients, making presentations to clients, and meeting with management. To demonstrate a match with your own prior work experience, if you have the relevant experience, you can state that you "currently provide strategic advice to clients," "facilitate work with members of the current management team," and "manage teamwork and make presentations to clients."

Constructing a Winning Résumé: An Insider's View

Certain pieces of critical advice are key to writing a winning résumé, regardless of whether a résumé is intended for a full-time business job, a summer job, a nonprofit job, or a legal job. What makes for a winning résumé? Eve Jaffe, president of Garb Jaffe & Associates Legal Placement of Los Angeles, California, and a prominent executive recruiter who has worked with graduates of top schools such as Stanford, UC–Berkeley, Harvard, and Yale, shares her insights:

A résumé is critically important, as it is the key to securing a job interview. A great candidate with a bad résumé will have difficulty securing any interviews. There are several keys to writing a winning résumé.

Succinctness and Information Placement. The résumé should be written clearly and succinctly, without excess wordiness. Get straight to the meat of the résumé, which is your experience and education. For candidates who have been out of school for five or fewer years, their education should be listed first with the educational institution at the top.

Clear Chronology. Dates of graduation are important to include. Sometimes I see older professionals leave off their dates of graduation because they feel uncomfortable about their age. I don't recommend doing this because it appears to be disingenuous and also makes the candidate appear lacking in confidence. Upon meeting a candidate, the employer will discover his or her approximate age anyway.

Honors Highlighted. If the candidate graduated in the top third of their class or higher, I recommend so stating on the résumé. Of course, the candidate should include any academic honors or activities as well.

Relevant and Valuable Experience Highlighted. The next section of the résumé is the experience section, listed in chronological order. The description of the candidate's experience should be tailored to fit the job for which he or she is applying. For instance, if the candidate is a professional who is applying for a securities job and has experience in three areas—mergers and acquisitions, lending/financing work, and securities—he or she should describe in detail his or her securities experience first, then include the other experience but with less description. It is not uncommon for a candidate to have two or three résumés tailored to the different positions for which he or she is applying. Candidates should not ramble on in the description of their experience. A good way to avoid doing this is to use bullet points. It will keep your descriptions short and to the point. It's also important for the interviewer to feel that the candidate has not held too many jobs. Therefore, leave off jobs held prior to school or during college (or simply list the company names and positions held, without job descriptions), unless you feel that those jobs continue to be important.

Adding an Extracurricular Touch. If the candidate has teaching experience, has been published, or holds an office in a relevant organization, those activities should be listed next in their own section. I also like to see an "interests" section at the bottom because it gives the interviewer a little insight into the type of person the candidate is and also provides conversation material for the interview outside of the standard professionally related discussion. If the candidate has a noteworthy hobby or activity in his or her past, it should be included. Interviewers love information about personal interests that demonstrate excellent qualities about a candidate.

Résumé Length. The rule of thumb for résumé lengths is one page, especially for candidates who have been out of school four years or less. Even for partners at firms, a résumé generally shouldn't be more than two pages. I once worked with a partner of a healthy book business who was very unhappy in his job. He had worked with another recruiter who sent his résumé all over town and couldn't get him more than a couple of interviews. When he showed me the résumé he had been using, it was five pages long! It was rambling and disorganized and included a list a quarter of a page long of different tasks he had done. He called that section "skills." Sections like this don't get read, and they make the candidate appear to be scattered and lacking writing skills. He was a terrific professional and business generator, but with a poorly written résumé, no one cared to meet him. I worked with him to pare his résumé down, to prioritize his achievements, to highlight relevant skills, and he was able to get multiple offers of employment.

Final Check

Before sending your résumé, be certain you have remained alert to the following ten things that often go wrong with résumé writing. Similarly, try to observe the résumé-writing dos listed that follow.

Top Ten Résumé Mistakes
- Résumé has too many job listings.
- Résumé lacks strategic arrangement of information: candidate's qualifications for available job not clear or prioritized.
- Résumé has too many bullet points per job listings—not adequately streamlined.
- Résumé lacks sense of direction or indicated progression of skills.
- Résumé lacks action verbs.
- Résumé contains typographical errors (typos).
- Résumé contains exaggerated information.
- Résumé lacks consistent formatting.
- Résumé does not explain missing years.
- Résumé is not professionally printed.

The Ultimate Résumé No-No: An Insider's View

Hong, of J. P. Morgan Chase, explains one of the deadliest interview sins:

The ultimate résumé no-no is a candidate's inability to explain in more detail what he or she has written down on the résumé. That's a deal killer. The interview will likely end there.

Top Ten Résumé Dos

- Elaborate in greater length about jobs that are most relevant to the position for which you are applying.
- Strategically arrange information, emphasizing your relevant skills and knowledge.
- Keep bullet points to five or six per job listing.
- Show a progression of skills over time.
- Use leadership language and action words.
- Do not exaggerate qualifications.
- Check résumé for typos or incorrect information.
- Account for any missing years somewhere on the résumé.
- Use consistent formatting.
- Have your résumé professionally or laser printed.

Know Your Résumé: Everything Is Fair Game

Finally, a frequent complaint heard among Fortune 100 recruiters is that many candidates show up with wonderful résumés but cannot back up the claims they make on their résumés. Inability to speak in depth about anything on your résumé is a sure way to lose a job opportunity. After compiling an effective résumé, therefore, be sure to observe all of these principles:

- **Remember that everything on your résumé is fair game.** The interviewer will feel free to ask you about anything you put on your résumé, so be able to speak about anything on your résumé in depth.
- **Do not exaggerate.** If an interviewer feels you have inflated your credentials, you could jeopardize your candidacy for a job.
- **Be sure you can relate the relevance of the résumé information.** With the exception of your extracurricular activities, which can simply reflect your personal interests, aim to relate the information on your résumé to your candidacy for the job you are applying for.

When you have finished composing your tailored résumé, it can become your effective tool for delivering an excellent interview, since it serves to guide, the interviewer to the key experiences, skills, and achievements. To help you know how to draw on your résumé and your record to deliver an excellent interview, the next two chapters are geared toward helping you speak about your record in ways that can help you deliver outstanding responses to common types of interview questions.

CHAPTER 4

DEMONSTRATE A FIT THROUGH YOUR RESPONSES TO KEY QUESTIONS

Now that you have guidelines to help you to create a résumé tailored to the specific job for which you will be applying, you should review how to deliver outstanding responses to questions in four key question areas: questions about your education, work experience, career goals, and personality or personal interests. In this chapter, we explore how you can project to the interviewer an image of yourself as a candidate with winning attributes. The chapter will then review specific tips for answering key types of questions.

Winning Attributes Recruiters Look For

Before attempting to answer questions in a job interview, you should clarify for yourself what sort of image you are seeking to put forward to the interviewer. You might wish for the interviewer to think of you in a few of these ways:

Goal-oriented
Hardworking
Dedicated
Determined
Focused

Motivated
Detail-oriented
Creative
Innovative
Analytical
Organized
Energetic
Articulate
Ethical
Trustworthy
Cooperative
One to take charge
Directed

Your Winning Profile

Which among these attributes should you focus on? Use two exercises to decide. First, think about which of these characteristics you have demonstrated in the past. You must be able to provide examples about how you have manifested these traits. Second, recognize that the best image or attributes of the ideal candidate will *vary by job*. With that in mind, review your assessment of the ideal attributes a candidate would have for your desired job (see pages 38–39). With that information, consider which three or four of your own attributes you would most like to convey to the interviewer as a part of the image you are putting forward.

For instance, if you are seeking to serve as a senior creative marketing director, it might be important to convey creativity, innovation, a willingness to take calculated risks, and analytical acumen (ability to assess your market well). If you are seeking to become a financial officer, it might be important to convey attributes such as goal orientation, detail orientation, organization, and high ethics. These examples demonstrate that the ideal candidate's attributes vary by job.

When thinking about how to present yourself in the interview, therefore, be sure to refer to your assessment on pages 38–39 of which attributes your potential employer would most value in a candidate. The

PERSONAL ATTRIBUTES WORK SHEET

Ideal Personal Attributes

_____

_____

_____

_____

My Strengths

_____

_____

_____

_____

Matches (Attributes That Appear in First and Second Sections)

_____

_____

_____

work sheet that follows, called Personal Attributes Work Sheet, can help you think through which of your personal attributes you should emphasize in your interview. To complete the Personal Attributes Work Sheet, rewrite the ideal personal attributes you identified on pages 38–39 in the first section. Then in the second section, write down the dominant attributes you have that are most relevant to the job. Compare those first two sections. Then, in the third section, write down the attributes that appear in both of the first two sections. This can help you decide which characteristics to highlight in your interview.

As you respond to questions in the four key areas described in this chapter, keep the winning attributes you want to emphasize in mind.

Take opportunities to convey those attributes through your responses when possible. Indeed, the key to answering questions excellently in an interview is to use each question as an opportunity to focus the interviewer on either your winning attributes or on the aspects of your education, work experience, or extracurricular record that demonstrate you are a match for the available job. Thus, be sure to also review your responses on pages 40–41 (the Professional Record Work Sheet), where you recorded the responsibility, tasks, and skills/knowledge you have that are relevant for the job you hope to secure. Keep those winning aspects of your record in the forefront of your mind, along with your winning attributes, as you respond to interview questions. The following examples illustrate how you can weave references to your winning attributes and references to your relevant experiences into your responses.

Mastering Responses to Educational Questions

If an interviewer asks you why you chose your major in college, you should use this question as an opportunity to demonstrate that you have attributes that are ideal and that you have attained relevant skills for your job through the major. When answering the question "In what ways did your major prepare you for this finance job?" Sheila responded:

> *As an economics major, when taking upper-level courses, I took two finance courses that gave me a solid foundation in finance concepts. That has helped prepare me. I also had to complete many mathematical courses as well as advanced economics classes that required extensive research and teamwork. All of those additional elements— mathematics, research, and teamwork—have also helped make me very prepared for my new finance career. In this field, the math skills, ability to work with data, and analytical skills that I have acquired will be keys to my success. Likewise, your company completes much of its work in teams and through research. The research skills and team skills I already have can therefore help me to excel at your company.*

In this answer, Sheila makes her major relevant not only in terms of content but also in terms of broader skills. That is a good blend. Sheila also could have used her response to draw attention to her winning attributes, in addition to pinpointing the ways in which her major has made her qualified for the available job. She could have remarked:

I loved my economics major, because I am someone who loves an intellectual challenge and who loves to problem solve in teams. My major suited my personality but also prepared me for a finance career. As an economics major, I took two finance courses that gave me a solid foundation in finance concepts. That has helped prepare me for this job. I also had to complete many math and economics classes that required extensive research and teamwork. Those were among my favorite aspects of my major. All of those additional elements—mathematics, research, and teamwork—have also helped make me very prepared for my new finance career because math and analytical skills are keys to success in the field of finance. Likewise, your company completes much of its work in teams and through research, so the research and team skills I have acquired can help me excel at your company.

Much of the substance of this response is the same as the prior example, but in this case Sheila took an extra effort to weave in references to her winning characteristics—her love of an intellectual challenge and her passion for problem solving. Because she also clarified how her major is relevant to finance, she did a great job of answering the question.

Even if you are applying for a business position without a business or economics background, you can still use this question as a chance to talk about your major in positive terms, emphasizing the broad skills that transcend a particular major and will enable you to distinguish yourself with excellent performance in a business position. Use this question as an opportunity to underscore your skills, knowledge, and experiences that will help you be an excellent employee. Emphasize transferable skills—skills that can be acquired in nonbusiness majors but that are relevant to business. Consider these examples of business-relevant transferable skills:

Relevance of Education: Ten Useful Types of Skills
1. Analytical skills
2. Problem-solving skills
3. Teamwork skills
4. Writing skills
5. Presentation skills
6. Mathematical skills
7. Computing skills
8. Research skills

WHY THIS INDUSTRY? THINGS TO CONSIDER

In interviews, it is common for you to be asked why you have chosen a particular industry or career. A best practice in answering this is to consider which characteristics are associated with your career or industry. Be prepared to demonstrate a fit between those characteristics and your own winning attributes. For instance, if a field is known for being fast-paced and characterized by innovation, be able to pinpoint how you have succeeded in fast-paced environments in the past and how you have demonstrated innovation and creativity. Here are some ways to think about the nature of your chosen industry:

➤ Degree of innovation
➤ Fast or slow pace
➤ Nature of intellectual activity within industry (technical, problem solving)
➤ Amount or type of new products
➤ Nature of work within (team-based, individualistic)
➤ Importance to lives of everyday people
➤ Impact on society
➤ Relation to other key sectors
➤ Lifestyle associated with

You should also be able to articulate "why this company" and "why this job."

9. Teaching skills

10. Persuasion skills

Chapter 8 illustrates in greater depth about how to communicate the relevance of transferable skills.

Mastering Responses to Questions About Work Experience

Questions about your work experience are usually central to any job interview. It is important, therefore, to learn how to deliver outstanding responses. When asking you about your work experience, the interviewer is asking you to draw parallels between your past work and your qualifications for the job you are interviewing for. You must demonstrate the relevance of your experience and clarify why you are qualified for the available job. For example, if the interviewer were to say, "Describe the job you held two years ago, before your current job," a good response is a concise, structured answer that conveys valued information about the skills and capabilities you used, developed, or refined during that job. In addition, answering this question gives you the opportunity to elaborate on your winning attributes and the activities and achievements that enabled you to move on to your current (and hopefully, more advanced) job. When asked this question, Andy answered:

> *In the job I held two years ago, my work as a junior manager included three main areas of responsibility. First, I was in charge of managing a team of five junior team members in completing a significant project for one of my company's core clients. This included setting goals for the team and assigning the specific roles and tasks of each team member. I also had to manage their work to ensure we were making headway toward our goals, and to provide guidance to my team members. Second, I was responsible for managing the company's relationship with that core client. This meant nurturing the relationship with the client by meeting individually with representatives and ensuring that our work was meeting their needs. Finally, I served as a liaison between*

the team and my superiors, so that they understood how things were progressing. My success as a junior manager opened up the opportunity to take a position as a full manager in my current job.

This answer is very structured, concise, and to the point. It presents a clear range of responsibilities that the interviewer will find directly relevant to the job offered.

In responding to the question about the job he held two years prior, Andy also could have chosen to weave in information about the personal attributes he wants to emphasize through his interview. For instance, Andy could have modified his response slightly to reply something like this:

I really enjoyed the job I held two years ago because I am someone who is very goal-oriented and enjoy leading groups. In addition, my job as junior manager helped me take steps toward my goal of managing a large department by providing me the opportunity to develop skills that could help me move toward my goal, such as good team leadership skills. In the job I held two years ago, my work included three main areas of responsibility. First, I was in charge of managing a team of five junior team members in completing a significant project for one of my company's core clients. This included setting goals for the team and assigning specific roles and tasks to each team member. I also had to manage my team members' work to ensure we were making headway toward our goals. Second, I was responsible for managing the company's relationship with that core client. This meant nurturing the relationship with the client by meeting individually with representatives and ensuring that our work was meeting their needs. Finally, I served as a liaison between the team and my superiors, so that my superiors understood how things were progressing. My success as a junior manager opened the opportunity for me to take a position as a full manager in my current job.

This response still conveys wonderful information about the skills and responsibilities that Andy had in a prior job that have helped make him qualified for the job he is now seeking. Additionally, Andy manages to weave in references to his winning characteristics—his goal orientation and his passion for leading teams. Those elements helped make this response a great use of the question about his prior work experience.

Mastering Responses to Questions About Your Goals

Discussions about your career goals are also often a part of many interviews. An interviewer who asks you about your goals is also assessing whether the goals you express match the opportunities presented by the advertised job. The interviewer also hopes to determine whether your ambitions are attractive to the organization. If the interviewer from a company that likes to hire long-term employees were to say, "Tell me about where you see yourself in five years," you might therefore choose to emphasize your goal-oriented nature and your desire to still be at their company making valued contributions in five years. In Bob's response, he chose to say:

> *In five years I hope to be serving as a manager of one of the restaurants in this chain. I love entrepreneurship and I am very goal oriented. I would enjoy the entrepreneurial challenge of building a strong branch and adapting marketing to the local environment so that my branch would become a high-revenue-earning one. My education has helped me prepare for this goal, by introducing me to broad principles of economics. And the fact that I have worked for a competitor chain gives me a good alternative perspective that I can draw on when working for your company. Because I have already served as a junior assistant manager and have experience building a successful staff and contributing to key marketing campaigns, I will bring a lot to the position of assistant manager and I believe I will be able to attain my career goals in your company.*

In this response the candidate conveys a medium-term goal that is compatible with the company's interests. The candidate also explains the relevance of his education and work experience to the job while also making reference to his winning attributes (goal-oriented nature and love of entrepreneurship).

WHY THIS FIRM? THINGS TO CONSIDER

Many interviewers want to hear you express why you want to work for their company rather than another. You should be able to express reasons for your choice. Here are characteristics you can cite when responding to why you prefer a particular company.

➤ Degree of innovation
➤ Fast or slow pace
➤ Nature of intellectual activity within (technical, problem solving)
➤ Types of products produced
➤ Work style (team based, individualistic)
➤ Types of clients served
➤ Corporate culture
➤ Characteristics of workforce (young, seasoned)
➤ Company's goal or mission

It is often effective to personalize your rationale for choosing the interviewing company. Make reference to your winning attributes. Thus, rather than just saying, "I like your company because its work is team-based and innovative," say, "I have always enjoyed team-based activities and I am very creative. Your company attracts me given the team-based, innovative nature of its work."

Conveying a Fit with the Organization—the Importance of Corporate Culture: An Insider's View

How do excellent interviewees and top MBAs convey a fit with the organization to which they are applying? Using largely informal networking structures—speaking with alumni or colleagues, for instance—skilled interviewees research the corporate culture of a firm to which they are applying and are able to demonstrate during the interview that their personality and goals are compatible with the culture of the interviewing company. Susan Kim, the head of the successful advisory group Kim, Hopkins & Associates—one of the largest franchises of American Express Financial Advisors in the Washington, D.C., area—explains the difference that demonstrating a fit can make both in securing and in retaining a job:

Ensuring that an employee is a good fit for your company is critical to corporate success, which is why many employers place great emphasis on it these days. For example, in my role as a senior financial adviser within the Fortune 100 company American Express, some of my clients work in high-level positions for consulting companies such as Booz Allen Hamilton, McKinsey & Company, and PriceWaterhouseCoopers. I can tell you, just by meeting a consultant, which of these companies they work for, because successful companies tend to ensure a match between their professionals and their culture. As I have grown my advisory group to over seven professionals with over $35 million under management, I have learned the importance of making sure there is a fit between a candidate and our culture, as it is critically important.

For example, I made the mistake once of choosing to hire the person with the fanciest résumé. It did not work out for us! He did not have the personality that fit with our organization. When we launched our new rapidly growing branch of American Express Financial Advisors two years ago, we wanted to build a team of the most dynamic, personable, dedicated individuals who shared our goals of excellent performance and excellent client service. Since we are a growing company, we needed a candidate, first and foremost, with similar goals and a personality compatible with the innovative professionals who form our staff. The ideal candidate needed to be eager to grow and to make more money; they needed to be someone who was not content with where they were. We failed to take that into consideration and chose the wrong candidate, because we were swayed by that candidate's sterling credentials alone. Today, we know better! We have sharpened our interviewing process, which has enabled us to staff a leading financial advisory team, becoming one of the largest American Express Financial Advisors franchises in the metropolitan D.C. area.

Now, as I interview, I ask a candidate, "What is an ideal work environment for you?" in order to sift through the candidates who are not a good fit for our organization. One candidate recently responded to that question with such precision and he so clearly demonstrated a fit that I hired him right away. He explained that he was looking for a work environment with a younger set of professionals who were intent on growing and were not content with just servicing their existing set of clients. He wanted an organization that cared about its clients. He wanted an organization known for excellence. I was struck; that was exactly what we offered and that was exactly the basis upon which we were trying to hire professionals! I hired him on the spot.

Mastering Responses to Questions About Personality and Personal Interests

Finally, some candidates fail to recognize that questions about personality or personal interests should also be used as opportunities to focus on winning attributes and present oneself as a suitable personality for the advertised job. For instance, if you are asked a question such as "What are your most memorable characteristics?" you should recognize this question as a chance to highlight key attributes and skills you bring to the new job. From your Job Assessment Work Sheet on pages 38–39 and your Personal Attributes Work Sheet, you should be aware of which qualities the ideal candidate would demonstrate and which of these you have. Spend time elaborating on your winning characteristics. For example, when answering a question about her memorable characteristics, Carla, a recent college graduate, said:

> *Overall, I am a very directed businessperson who has been building a strong skill set in marketing in order to attain my career goal of serving the marketing department of a company like yours. My most memorable characteristics are creativity, hard work, and a friendly personality. The importance of my creativity can be seen as I helped launch a new club during college, which grew to be one of the largest on campus by my senior year. My creativity can also be seen through my success in leading two new marketing campaigns at my current company. My hard work has been demonstrated through the success of*

those marketing campaigns. And my friendly personality has mani-
fested itself both through my community work and through my team
leadership at work. I know others enjoy working with me, which is one
reason why my marketing teams do so well.

This answer does a great job of focusing on three attributes that are directly relevant to Carla's ability to be an effective and pleasant marketing professional to work with. Carla provides examples for each attribute offered, and she uses the opportunity to focus attention on her successes.

The Art of Responding to Personality and Fit Questions: An Insider's View

How are skilled interviewees able to respond excellently to personality or fit questions during an interview? Byron, a Harvard graduate with experience at the top consulting firms McKinsey & Company and Booz Allen Hamilton, uses his experience as a successful hire and his interaction with graduates from MBA and law school programs such as those at Harvard, Stanford, and Yale to provide insights about best practices to employ in order to interview excellently:

In order to present excellent responses to personality or fit questions such as "Describe yourself in three adjectives," or "Describe what you are looking for in a firm," you must first have an understanding of the culture of the firm to which you are applying. For instance, in leveraging your contacts, you might find that the culture of the company to which you are applying is not very casual in terms of dress—so definitely attend the interview in a suit! You might also discover that the company is flexible in terms of work hours and encourages its professionals to pursue hobbies outside of work. The culture of a company can include whether it is very family oriented, whether it is a work-all-night shop, whether its main projects are team based, whether the attire is casual or formal, etc. Network with friends, colleagues, or even a company representative at a job fair to gain an understanding of corporate culture. Speaking with junior-level professionals in the organization can also be helpful, if you are able to get a business card and speak with someone before the interview. Once you have this knowledge, you can craft your answers more appropriately to reflect a fit with the company.

I advise discreetly integrating references to the corporate culture in ways that show a fit. If the company is known for assertiveness, talk about how you are a leader and enjoy exploring new ideas. If the company is known for being family oriented, make reference to your activities with your family. Many leading companies take the "fit" issue very seriously. If you cannot blend into the new work environment, you will likely not be successful. So do your homework and prepare your responses to fit questions appropriately.

Value of the Memorable Answer: An Insider's View

Glenn Jaffe, a senior vice president at a Fortune 100 company, warns against clichés:

I look for pointed and catchy responses with a foundation of candor behind them. Most interviewers have made up their minds in the first five minutes of the interview. When asked to tell about oneself, I would hope that a candidate would endeavor to differentiate, to stand out, to make a memorable statement. It is only the strong interviewee that has the courage and initiative to respond to a question with a truly memorable answer.

All Things Equal, a Fire in the Eye

Finally, a word about enthusiasm. Throughout all this, don't forget the importance of enthusiasm! Many Fortune 100 recruiters report that, all things equal, they will choose the candidate who demonstrated a high level of enthusiasm or "fire in the eye" for the job. That is, they choose to work with the candidate who is truly excited about the new job. Enthusiasm can make a strong, positive impression.

CHAPTER 5

SHAPE THE INTERVIEW WITH RESPONSES TO OPEN-ENDED AND TURNAROUND QUESTIONS

One of the key best practices in interviewing excellently is the ability to take control of the interview or shape the direction of the interview. In an interview, you have a wonderful opportunity to shape the direction of the interview when you are asked an open-ended or non-specific question, such as "Tell me about yourself" or "How would others characterize you?" The open-ended question differs from specific questions such as "What courses in calculus did you complete?" because a specific question requires a specific answer for an adequate response.

Many professionals tell me they get very nervous when asked an open-ended question in an interview. Their general reaction is, "What am I supposed to say? I have no idea where to start." If you are well prepared, an open-ended question is one of the best questions you can receive in an interview. This chapter will help you understand how you can use the open-ended question to present yourself in a good light. It also explores how to create and address turnaround questions.

The Gift of the Open-Ended Question

In an interview, the interviewer is often trying to ask questions that allow him or her to paint a picture of you, so the interviewer can assess whether you will be a good employee and whether you fit well with the organization. The reason the open-ended question is such a wonderful gift in an interview is that it is as if an interviewer has handed you the paintbrush and has given you permission to paint the picture yourself. You are able to control the colors of the paint, the strokes of the brush, the emphasis of the details. It is an ideal situation.

To use this ideal situation to the best of your abilities, you must go into the interview knowing what top three or four attributes you want the interviewer to associate with you before you leave. You must also know what top three to five accomplishments you want the interviewer focused on when considering your record of achievement. When you are asked an open-ended question, you can move the conversation directly to a discussion of those attributes and those achievements. Here's how.

Addressing Open-Ended Questions Effectively

- Use the question to paint a picture of your winning three or four qualities—the ones that will demonstrate a match between your qualities and those of the ideal candidate.
- Use the question to move straight to the strengths that distinguish you—the skills and work experience that show you are highly qualified for the job.

Using Open-Ended Questions to Paint a Picture of Yourself

Consider an instance when a job candidate, Peter, is interviewing for a position as a manager of a small computer consulting company. The interviewer has asked Peter to "tell me about yourself." This is an example of a poor answer:

I was born in Kansas City and lived there until I was twelve. I moved to Chicago at that time, and I lived with my parents in Chicago until I went to college at the University of Chicago. At that time, I moved to a campus apartment and majored in economics. I spent my junior year abroad in Scotland and then returned to the University of Chi-cago. After finishing my senior year, I took a position at a computer store, where I have worked for four years. Now I am looking to move into a company with a broader client base so that I can expand my skills.

Now, clearly, that answer is not horrible. Peter was able to convey after a few sentences a sense of why he is interested in a job with the computer consulting company. But even though the response is not hor-rible, it clearly is not very strategic and does not take advantage of the opportunity to focus the conversation on his most attractive attributes and achievements. Equally important, in the first few sentences, Peter simply recites some information that the interviewer likely has in Peter's résumé. What was the point of that? That repetition of biographical details, in this instance, was not an optimal use of the time and the answer.

Once he took the time to prepare, Peter was able to deliver a much stronger answer in an interview at a later date. This time, when asked the question, "Tell me about yourself?" Peter answered:

I am a very goal-oriented person with a passion for new ideas and a desire to achieve excellent outcomes in all that I do. I have demonstrated my commitment to excellence in many ways. For instance, when I attended the University of Chicago, I earned a B+ average in a very difficult major, and I graduated with honors. I was recruited by a lead-ing computer company in our city, and my experience there reinforced my passion for new ideas. My innovation and contributions resulted in three promotions in four years and an award of "Employee of the Year" last year. I now have a very valuable skills set and am ready to move to the next level of my career, working as a manager. That is why I have approached your computer consulting company. I believe this is my ideal company and job position.

Many things make this answer a much better use of the open-ended question. Among the most important are these. First, Peter uses his very first sentence to characterize himself with words that convey a sense of initiative, drive, goal orientation, and excellence. These are all attributes the employer will value. By painting himself in this light, Peter has probably caused the interviewer to sit up in his or her seat with deep interest. Second, Peter moved directly to a discussion of some of the achievements that will mark him as stronger than some of the other job applicants. These achievements may also form the basis for why the employer may choose him over other applicants. Emphasizing his academic achievement assures the interviewer that Peter has the skills to make a good contribution in the new organization if he is hired. Emphasizing his promotions and award for excellence not only underscores that his company recognized him as a high-performing employee, but also hints that through his promotions, Peter has gained greater responsibilities and greater skills, so he is ready to "move to the next level" of his career. Finally, this answer is wonderful because Peter ends with a sentence that might prompt the interviewer to ask a follow-up question. By stating, "I believe this is my ideal company and job position," the interviewer might choose to expand on that end remark by asking a question such as "Why do you believe this company and position are ideal for you?" Thus, Peter has set himself up for a follow-up question that will allow him to elaborate even further about his skills and the many ways he is a good match for the company and the position.

This example demonstrates that an open-ended question is a fantastic opportunity to carve out the direction of the interview. An open-ended question can be used to your advantage if you move into the interview with a firm understanding of the attributes and accomplishments you seek to convey to the interviewer. Suppose Karen, a recent college graduate, is applying for a position as a store manager for a national clothing chain. She has already considered what attributes she would like to convey to the interviewer. She is highly disciplined and organized, enjoys interacting with people, is creative, and loves a challenge. Before the interview, she also outlined the activities of her college years that illustrate these attributes. When she receives a job interview, the interviewer asks her a open-ended question: "Why did you attend your chosen college?" For the unprepared interviewee, this would be a less than ideal response:

> *I did not want to travel too far from home, since I am relatively close to my parents, so I looked for an affordable university within fifty miles of my home. I didn't have many other choices in the area, and the college I attended had a fairly good reputation, so I chose to go there. The experience was very pleasant.*

That sounds like a truthful answer, but this answer does little to enhance the image of the interviewee in the eyes of the interviewer. While it is wonderful to care about one's parents, this could have been answered much more strategically.

Because Karen went into the interview prepared, she has a response that positions her much better in the eyes of the interviewer. Karen has been looking for opportunities in the interview to weave in information about her winning characteristics. When asked, "Why did you attend your chosen college?" Karen notes this is an opportunity and responds this way:

> *I am a very creative person who enjoys interacting with people and a challenge. My college gave me what I was looking for by enabling me to challenge myself with a terrific curriculum, use my creativity in class projects, and develop excellent leadership skills as I interacted with others in the club I founded, the Environmental Club. One of the things I enjoyed most in college was my major, economics. It was rigorous and demanding, and it really made me challenge my thinking and become much more disciplined in my work. The experience of completing difficult problem sets on a weekly basis and completing a detailed thesis on a world event also made me very organized in my use of time. I made a good choice when I chose my college.*

What makes this response excellent is that Karen touched on her key attributes while also mentioning one of the achievements that distinguish her record—her leadership in the Environmental Club. She has successfully portrayed herself as a hard worker who is creative and thrives amid rigorous, challenging experiences. The image she has established in the interviewer's mind is positive and attractive.

Creating Turnaround Questions and Responding to Them

In an interview, you also have a wonderful opportunity to shape the content of the interview when you are asked a question that can be transformed into a "turnaround" question. By this, I mean you can strategically address a question that asks you to talk about a negative experience you've had or about one of your negative personal qualities. By skillfully "turning around" such questions, you will create the chance to elaborate on some of your most valuable experiences and qualities.

Turning Around Questions About Your Failures

To demonstrate, take the case of Eleana who was interviewing for a teaching job and was asked to elaborate on her greatest failure as a teacher in her current junior high school class. Eleana, unprepared for this question, blurts out one of the first examples she thinks of. She responds:

> *One of the biggest failures was my inability a year ago to motivate my class to study well enough to pass the school-wide English exam that our principal administered to ensure that students were gaining the basic skills they would need to proceed on to high school. It was a disappointment, but that class represented a very difficult group of students. I remind myself that there were other tests on which they performed very well, and those students even passed a statewide English exam later that same year. But my failure to motivate them to pass my principal's exam was significant for me. I intend to successfully encourage my students to do better in my next teaching position. I am very certain I have the skills to do so.*

Certainly, there are a couple of positive aspects to this response. Eleana displays some confidence in her abilities as she states "I am very certain I have the skills" to encourage students in the future to pass school-wide English exams. But this positive comment does not adequately offset the many negative aspects of Eleana's answer. In particular, two aspects of Eleana's response are troubling. First, Eleana indicated that she had failed to enable her students to pass an exam that was designed to test basic skills. There may be circumstances that explain why Eleana failed in this task—perhaps her students were simply a boisterous bunch of kids who would have been difficult for any teacher to handle. But an interviewer might likely read this admission by Eleana as an indictment of her ability to perform well as a teacher. Even though Eleana points out that there were other exams on which the students performed well, the interviewer would tend to believe that if the school-wide exam was not reflective of the abilities of her students, she would not have dwelled on the failure and therefore would not have chosen to bring it up as a great failure.

Because this answer undercuts one of the most important skills that Eleana needs to establish in the interview—her ability to excel through excellent teaching skills—her response is a poor choice for this question. Similarly, even though Eleana expresses confidence that she can perform better in the future, a potential employer would be more comfortable hiring Eleana if he or she were certain of her record of success in her current job.

Bearing these mistakes in mind, it is possible to see that there is a better approach for answering "failure" questions such as this. A best practice is to use a turnaround technique. That is, address the failure question posed only briefly, with a short synopsis of a failure. In the case of "Tell me about your greatest professional failure," you should devote only a small part of your response to providing details about the failure. It is a weak spot in your credentials, so there is no need to prolong the discussion about the failure. Rather, acknowledge the failure quickly, so as to answer the question, but quickly transition your response to speak about the lessons you learned, and how you have achieved many successes since the failure.

There are other useful guidelines for determining what topic to elaborate on. If the interviewer does not specifically ask for you to elaborate on a failure from your work experience, choose a non–work-related experience that has little bearing on the skills or knowledge you must use excellently to excel in your potential new job. In that way, the failure you elaborate on will not call your work-related credentials into question. Also, if you are able to elaborate on a failure that is further back in time, rather than more recent, that is often a better choice. After all, your aim is to turn around the question quickly and then elaborate on how you have succeeded since the failure by employing the lessons that you learned from your failure. Do not choose a failure that is too recent, because in that case you will have a hard time elaborating on your successes since the failure; it will simply be the case that enough time has not yet passed for you to have established a record of success since your failure. Finally, don't elaborate on a failure that was very costly to your employer. If you do so, the interviewer will likely become nervous, wondering whether you would make a similar costly mistake at their organization.

Let's return to Eleana's case. Once she learned these best practices, she was much more prepared to answer failure questions and to turn them around, creating opportunities to talk about her successes. In another interview, therefore, when asked about her greatest failure in her current position as a junior high school teacher, Eleana replied:

When I first started teaching four years ago, I was not aware that I would have such a broad range of abilities represented among my students. I started with a one-size-fits-all approach to teaching. Soon, I saw that some students were left behind because the pace seemed too quick, and others were frustrated by the slow pace. While the majority of students were in the middle, I felt that I owed it to my students to help them all learn. My lack of ability to do this during the first months of my new position was a failure. I took the time to speak with other teachers to understand how they dealt with similar situations. I learned from them good practices for teaching a class of students with such a wide range of abilities. Since that time, I have been able to teach my students in a way that allows each of them to learn according to their abilities. My students have learned and they have performed excellently on their exams.

This was a much better choice. Eleana chose a topic further back in time, and quickly turned the failure question into an opportunity to talk about the lessons she learned and how she has become a better teacher.

The turnaround method of responding to questions is useful with a variety of questions. Consider using this turnaround technique when addressing questions such as "Tell me about your greatest setback in life," "Tell me about your greatest personal failure," or "Tell me about a time you were disappointed in yourself."

Greatest Failure Questions: What to Avoid
- A failure that is too recent
- An example that was financially costly to your employer
- An example that cost your employer a client or hurt your employer's reputation
- A failure that is central to your current work
- A failure that reflects a weakness in the skills you need to use excellently to succeed in your potential new job
- An example where you cannot elaborate on what you have learned
- An example where you cannot cite another example of when you dealt with a similar situation and succeeded

Greatest Failure: Sample Approach
- Spend only a small amount of your response addressing your failure.
- Talk about the lessons you learned.
- Spend the remainder of your time mentioning an example of when you succeeded by applying the lessons you learned from the failure you have spoken about.

Turning Around Questions About Your Weaknesses

Another type of question that you should view as a turnaround opportunity is a question about your greatest weakness. Just like questions about your greatest failures, many candidates are uncomfortable answering questions about weaknesses, because they do not know what to say. Some people feel that if they mention something like "I work too hard," they will have just offered a generic answer that is not very satisfying for the interviewer. What is a best practice? Be cautious. It is better to offer a more generic answer than to respond by pointing out a weakness that makes the interviewer question your qualifications for the available job.

Consider the case of Nathan, who chose not to be cautious in his response to an interview question about his greatest professional weakness. He answered by pinpointing one of several weaknesses of which he was aware:

> *In my position as a manager at my bank, one of my greatest professional weaknesses is that I do not communicate with my subordinates as best as I can. Given my personality, I personally always prefer to hear criticism in a straightforward and uncoated fashion. But when I issue that sort of to-the-point criticism to my subordinates, they react very defensively and it has caused some friction. But otherwise, my work as a manager has been very effective and I believe I can be a great manager at your company.*

This answer, while not necessarily poor enough to cost the candidate a job opportunity, could have been much stronger. First, Nathan has indicated that his actions cause friction at work. He makes no attempt to indicate that he has tried to smooth the friction over, or even that it is a priority for him to smooth it over and create a more harmonious work environment. In many cases, interviewers do not want to hire managers who cause friction in the workplace unnecessarily or who do not attempt to create harmonious work relations after some friction has been introduced. Nathan has probably caused the interviewer to question whether he is a difficult person to work with. Also, in his response, Nathan does not indicate that he is working to improve his greatest professional weakness. That is a problem in and of itself. If you are aware of a professional weakness, the interviewer will want to know that you are proactive enough to be diligently seeking to strengthen that weakness. Here is how Nathan could have answered this question better. He could have responded:

When I first took up my position as a manager at my bank, one of my greatest professional weaknesses was that I did not communicate with my subordinates as best as I could have. Given my personality, I personally always prefer to hear criticism in a straightforward fashion. But when I issue that sort of to-the-point criticism to my subordinates, they react very defensively and it has caused some friction. I know that as a manager, my role is not only to manage our work excellently but also to motivate my workers to improve their performance. If I was demotivating my workers with such direct criticism, then that indicated to me that I had a weakness in my communication style. Now, I always remind myself not to issue abrasive or uncoated criticism. Even though I would not mind receiving criticism like that, this style does not work for my subordinates. I have worked since that early period of my role as a manager to adapt my style and to combine a mixture of praise and constructive criticism. Not only is our work environment very harmonious now, but I am pleased to see my subordinates respond positively to my feedback of their performances.

That is a much better response. Nathan points out a weakness, demonstrates that he has actively addressed it (and continues to do so), and also indicates that the initial friction that his old style introduced has been resolved.

Greatest Weakness Questions: What to Avoid
- A weakness that resulted in a bad outcome that proved financially costly to your employer
- A weakness that resulted in a bad outcome that cost your employer a client or hurt your employer's reputation
- A weakness that indicates a problem using the skills you will need to excel in your potential new job
- A weakness that indicates a significant skill needed for the central work in your current job

- An example upon which you cannot elaborate to describe how you are productively addressing and strengthening that weakness

Now that you are aware of some of the best practices for responding to open-ended questions, you can use them as opportunities to convey the winning attributes and work experience that the interviewer will most value. Similarly, now that you have learned how to turn around questions about your shortcomings, weaknesses, or failures, you can use turnaround questions to convey information about your ability to learn and about your strengths. With this information, you can now respond excellently to open-ended and turnaround questions.

CHAPTER 6

ADDRESS CLEAR WEAKNESSES (WITHOUT APOLOGIZING!)

One situation that often causes anxiety among job candidates is the knowledge that they have a clear weakness they must address during the interview. A clear weakness can take many forms, such as a low GPA, a bad standardized-test score (some employers request your SAT score or graduate-level standardized-test result), or a disciplinary problem that is noted on a transcript. There are important ways to handle excellently a discussion about a clear weakness during an interview. First, and very important, don't be defensive when addressing the concern. Be willing to acknowledge the clear weakness. If you become defensive, the interviewer will likely assume you are unable to handle criticism well or are "hardheaded" and don't like to admit it when you have made a mistake. This is likely to hurt you in the interview.

Second, don't apologize for the clear weakness. Normally, an apology will be seen as reflecting low self-confidence. Ideally, your response should be somewhere between these two extremes of becoming defensive and apologizing. With an even tone, you should simply acknowledge the weakness and then move the conversation toward your successes.

This is the third key to handling a discussion about a clear weakness. After acknowledging your clear weakness in an open, level tone, quickly move the conversation to a discussion of other aspects of your record that can demonstrate you have either addressed or overcome that weakness. The fact is, we all experience challenging situations and circumstances, and the interviewer is no different. Therefore, most interviewers will be somewhat receptive to you if you acknowledge your clear weakness and then demonstrate how you have addressed it.

The rest of this chapter elaborates on how to handle questions about various clear weaknesses.

Poor Grades in a Few Classes

All of us go through difficult times, and many of us are stronger in some subjects than in others. If you have a low grade point average, it is often less of an obstacle to overcome in the interviewing process if only a few grades lowered the GPA. In that case, often the courses with low grades are the same sort of courses. For instance, if you are weak as a writer, you might have received low grades in all of your college writing courses. When your low grades are confined to a specific subject, you can present a stronger case by emphasizing that you are applying for a job that does not depend on skills in that particular area. Your strategy should be to point out how strong your grades are in all other areas, particularly in the areas that are more relevant to the job you are applying for.

Similarly, a low GPA is less of an obstacle if your low grades are concentrated in a particular period of time. Generally, your strategy in this case should be to point out how your grades have improved over time if you were affected by a negative experience.

Consider the instance of Mark, who has a low GPA because he was not focused during his first two years of college. Mark became much more organized and motivated in his last two years of college and during his professional work. In spite of this, he knows his low GPA may be a concern in the interview. He is ready for the question about his GPA when the interviewer looks at his transcript and says, "We are really concerned that your low GPA indicates both lack of commitment and lack of discipline." Mark responds without defensiveness in a way that acknowledges the low GPA but emphasizes his strengths:

Yes, my GPA was low during my first two years of college. At that time, I was adjusting to the new college environment and trying to learn to balance the demands of my schoolwork with my part-time job. But I was not one to give up prematurely. I was determined to make the adjustment and develop the skills and time management abilities that could enable me to eventually excel in college. Once I became more adjusted to the new environment and challenges, I focused my energies, and my grades improved dramatically. In my last two years, you will note that I earned a B+ average in the advanced courses I was taking, and I also began to distinguish myself in campus politics. My classmates elected me to the student government, which was a tremendous honor. I am hoping that you will note how much my grades improved in my last two years and that you will see the notable improvement in my overall record during those last years as signs of my determination to meet and overcome challenges. My last two years in college are much more accurate indicators of my future success than the first two years were.

This response was well-articulated and convincing. No doubt, Mark left a great impression and the interviewer was more prone to overlook the two years of poor academic performance.

Poor Overall GPA

Consider next the situation of Sarah, who was unfocused throughout her entire college career. This is a harder situation to deal with, but once Sarah establishes a record of success after college, she will be able to address her lack of performance in college with greater ease. When asked about her low GPA in college, which started off low in year one and did not improve before graduation, Sarah replied confidently:

Yes, my GPA is low. Unfortunately, when I attended college, I was not very focused on my studies. I viewed college as a time to explore different ideas and interests. I became involved in many clubs and made significant contributions to several, including one involved with the homeless. It was only after I left college and entered the work world that I realized I had made such a mistake in neglecting my studies. Once I found a job that captured my interests, I focused my energies and excelled. I am hoping that you will therefore consider my record since college, which reflects much more accurately my commitment and discipline. Since I have served as an assistant manager, I have excelled, helping our client base to grow. My reviews have been excellent, and I was promoted just last year.

Poor Grades: When You Might Have to Wait It Out

Granted, some jobs are highly technical or depend on strong analytical skills. In those instances, attempting to explain your poor GPA may not work. Your better strategy may be to secure a job related to your longer-term career that is easier to land without a higher GPA—one in which college academic performance is not a primary basis of employee selection. Once you excel in that job, you will be establishing a strong record of achievement that you can point to when you try to later secure your dream job. At times, therefore, you must put in a couple of years between a poor record and your dream job. After doing so, employing Sarah's strategy of pointing to the new record of achievement will likely prove successful for you. As an alternative, you can consider enrolling in a one-year degree program or take courses in the area of your weakness. If you perform well, you can point to your new record of achievement during the interview, and your prior record should become less of an obstacle.

Poor Standardized-Test Results

Some highly technical jobs require that you supply standardized-test scores to hiring personnel in order to provide another metric for the employers to use when determining if you are suitable for a job. Some job candidates may therefore need to explain a poor standardized-test score. This is easiest to do when there is a marked difference between your test score and your performance in school.

Take the example of Janet, who received a poor standardized-test score but managed to excel in college. She went into her job interview prepared to address her test score. When the topic came up, she addressed it strategically—acknowledging the low score but quickly focusing the conversation on the many other metrics that could be used to attest to her strong analytical abilities. When asked about her low score, she replied this way:

> *Yes, my standardized-test score is low. This is not an indication of my lack of motivation or my lack of preparation for the exam. I spent months preparing, but I have never been a strong standardized-test taker. Luckily, my inability to score well on such exams did not deter me from gaining admission to an excellent college, and you can see how I distinguished myself in college with a high GPA. I hope that you can feel assured of my ability to handle quantitative tasks, given my performance in the math and engineering courses I took. In my performance at my last job, which included working with financial statements and complex data sets, my performance ratings were always in the highest category also, which indicates that I mastered the key quantitative skills needed.*

Disciplinary Issues

Disciplinary issues represent a more difficult challenge to address in the interview process, simply because they are a red flag to the interviewer that at one time in your life you had difficulty making the right ethical decision or behaving in a manner that the interviewer would consider upstanding. For any organization, the consequences of hiring an employee who lacks high ethical standards or engages in behavior that calls for disciplinary action could be grave. Such a candidate will appear to be a risky choice for a position. You therefore will need to present to the interviewer a convincing argument about how you have changed since the period during which you received the disciplinary action.

While difficult, this is possible. The best way to make a convincing case that you have changed is to build a record that reinforces this notion. You must build a record that demonstrates your high ethics, shows you engaging in upstanding behavior, and illustrates clearly that you have learned a lesson and would not repeat the behavior that merited the disciplinary action. I have seen many instances where a candidate has presented a compelling case that convinced interviewers that the candidate's disciplinary problems of the past would stay in the past.

Consider the case of John, who was caught cheating on a college exam and was expelled from college for a year. The disciplinary action appeared on his transcript, and John was prepared when asked about this during an interview. He responded with this explanation:

The biggest mistake I have made in my life was engaging in dishonest behavior on that exam. It was foolish, and there is no excuse for it. During the year I was away from college as a result of that choice, I took the time to really do some thinking about my values, my ambitions, and how I would need to change in order to do something meaningful with my talents. During that year, I began to work more in community projects, and I also began to mentor young people who were having difficulty. I found it rewarding to be able to share my experiences—positive and negative—in ways that could help others avoid the mistake I made in college. I have continued that work, and I intend to continue it in the future.

When I returned to school the next year, I felt like a new person. I went to the professor whose class I was in when I made my mistake, and I apologized. He was impressed with my turnaround and even allowed me to reenroll in his class. I received a strong grade, as you can see. After returning to school, my grades were high. This experience turned out to be a wonderful opportunity to learn and change, and I carry with me the strong ethical values that have enabled me to succeed since that time.

CHAPTER 7

PRESENT A STRONG EXPLANATION IF YOU'VE BEEN OUT OF WORK

Given the turbulent economic times of the past few years, many people have found themselves out of work, some for short periods, others for longer periods. If you find that you have a gap to account for in your work experience, you are not alone. This chapter outlines ways you can address gaps in your work during a job interview, as well as ways in which you can use your time out of the workforce constructively and valuably.

How to Deal with Periods of Unemployment

If you were out of work for only a couple of months, normally you do not need to explain this during an interview. The interviewer will often be content to hear that you took the time to assess where you hoped to go with your career, research companies and job opportunities, and prepare to begin interviewing. However, if you have been out of work for a longer period of time—more than four months, for instance—you are best off if you can state to your interviewer that you were doing more with that time than searching for a job. An employer wants to see that you were not content to sit idle but took the initiative to use the time off as a tremendous opportunity. Ways to do this include expanding your professional qualifications through certifications, expanding your knowledge base, deepening your professional experiences or your ideas about your long-term goals, and broadening your worldview through travel.

This chapter outlines various strategies for impressing your interviewer with the activities you engaged in during your time off.

What to Do if Unemployed: An Insider's View

Edward, a manager at IBM, advises that while being unemployed is no crime, selective companies do like to see initiative even during down times:

The best practice can be summarized as "keep moving!" Every one of us has things we want to do but we could not do it because we were working and did not have time. Well, an unemployed person has the time to pursue such activities. I do not like it when a candidate just keeps standing still waiting for a job.

Enhance Your Professional Qualifications

One of the ways in which you can impress a potential employer is to say that during your time off, you took the opportunity to enhance your skills and qualifications by attaining certifications and licenses. Obtaining these credentials can deepen your knowledge in your career area while also making you more attractive to the customers or clients of your prospective new employer. For example, if you work in financial planning, you could study for and obtain another license, such as the Series 7 broker's license. If you are a corporate lawyer who is out of work, you might take the opportunity to secure a real estate license, which can deepen your knowledge about real estate transactions. If you are a computer specialist, you might want to get additional certifications in computing, such as C++ certification. For those in other fields, you should determine whether there are certifications in your field that can enhance your skills and knowledge.

Deepen Your Knowledge

For many people, it is difficult to find the money or the time to secure a new license or certification. Another alternative is to deepen your knowledge by taking courses online, at a junior college, or through an extension school of a university. You can likely locate a course for as little as $100 at a junior college. If you work as an administrative assistant, for instance, you might want to take a course in management processes at a local junior college. If you work as a store manager, you might want to take a course in marketing. Taking a course enables you to tell an interviewer that you turned a setback (being laid off) into an opportunity, gaining valuable knowledge through formal instruction.

Enhance Your Work Experiences

If you are affected by a prolonged period of unemployment, for as long as a year for instance, it is best to be able to indicate that you continued to put your skills to use in some socially useful fashion. I have met many consultants at large consulting firms who suffered from downsizing in recent years, given the economic downturn. Rather than sit idle, they began to offer consulting services for low or no fees to nonprofit organizations or small businesses. In doing so, they were able to apply their existing business and team management skills. In addition, they were able to develop key entrepreneurial skills as they marketed their services, set pricing, developed attractive services, and success-

---

YOU'VE BEEN FIRED: NOW WHAT?

➤ **Your own consulting company:** Use the time to run your own business, even if on a pro bono (unpaid) basis, showing your desire to apply and stretch your skills.

➤ **More credentials:** Use the time to enhance your expertise and credentials through certifications or licenses.

➤ **Deeper expertise:** Use the time to refine your knowledge through online or extension courses.

➤ **Long-term goals:** Use the time to conduct research into your desired long-term goals.

➤ **Travel:** Use the time to travel and experience other cultures.

➤ **Community service:** Use the time in community service, to enhance the nonwork aspects of your résumé.

fully implemented projects. All of these steps can be seen as pluses on a résumé.

If you worked as an administrative assistant and were laid off, you might offer your services to small nonprofit organizations, helping them consider ways to organize themselves more effectively. To a future employer, taking this sort of initiative will likely be seen as demonstrating excellent personal characteristics.

Broaden Your Worldview

It is also acceptable to take the time during a period of unemployment to travel. Today's business world is globalizing and is characterized by diversity. Becoming more versed in the many cultures in the United States and around the world can be seen as positive. Therefore, there is little reason to be bashful about taking a break between jobs to travel and expand your understanding of the world around you and of the many cultures around you. I have worked with many successful candidates who traveled throughout Asia, Latin America, Africa, or some other region of interest during a period of time off. They used those enriching experiences to impress a new employer. Others who chose to travel around the United States have been able to use those experiences to their advantage. They were able to convey to an interviewer how much history they learned about their own state or region of the country, and how much they learned about the many cultures in various regions of the country.

Using Time out of Your Career to Enhance Your Candidacy: An Insider's View

In today's economy, many talented workers have lost their jobs and have experienced long periods of unemployment. If you are interviewing for a job after months of unemployment, what will an interviewer want to see on your résumé in terms of how you have used your time out of the workforce? What do employers view as constructive ways of using time off? Celeste Garcia, a professional with a bachelor's and a master's degree from Harvard University, became a senior-level consultant with PricewaterhouseCoopers and now serves as managing director of consulting services for the D.C.-based Ivy Planning Group consulting firm. Here, she shares the best practices she has learned through her successful career. She also provides insights into what impresses her as she interviews top MBAs for jobs today:

There are many ways to use time out of the workforce creatively and constructively. When I interviewed candidates both at PricewaterhouseCoopers and at Ivy Planning Group, my antennae would go up if there were unexplained gaps on a résumé. If the candidate is currently unemployed, it raises questions: Why hasn't this person gotten a job? What happened at the last job? You do not want your interviewer to see a period of unemployment as a big red flag, so you need to take steps to mitigate the influence of a gap on your résumé. Here are some good steps to take and a few things to avoid:

Participate in projects. Many professionals will fill their time during unemployment with ad hoc jobs. Put those down on your résumé as projects, and explain clearly what skills you employed and which skills you further developed through work on those projects. That can impress an employer or make the gap less obvious.

Engage in meaningful volunteer work. Volunteer work is also a good way to use your time to contribute and also to possibly gain new skills. You can volunteer to help lead or organize a conference that is taking place in your career field. You can undertake pro bono work for a meaningful institution. You can take a course—but make sure that it is a thoughtful choice of a course, something that provides you with concrete skills or knowledge. You can participate in projects with the government. I know a candidate who took on a consulting project for the government of a developing country and was able to write about that excellently on his résumé. I was impressed! Another candidate explained how she had used her organizational skills to run a conference during a period of unemployment. Those activities can impress an interviewer.

Put the reasons for your unemployment in context. If you were terminated or lost your job because of mass layoffs, make that clear in your conversation with an interviewer (good people get laid off). Even better, references from your prior place of employment help mitigate any concerns by demonstrating that your loss of employment was not performance based. In the event that you did not get terminated but you simply grew tired and wanted a break, make that clear. That is fine—people sometimes work too hard and need time out. But in that situation, it is important that you have strong references from your prior employer and that you can draw on those references during the interview process.

Avoid overt negativity. Be careful how you frame your comments about your prior employer. When I meet a candidate who speaks negatively about his or her current or former employer, I wonder if they will do this to me and our firm. Such behavior calls people's judgment into question. Be diplomatic in what you say.

Using Time Off Creatively: An Insider's View

Given the ups and downs of the current market, it is not unusual to find that an excellent professional suffered a job loss and has been out of work for months. In that situation, an interviewer will often still probe to make sure nothing is amiss. How can you assure that potential employer that your unemployment is not a big red flag? Here's an answer from Rajat, a banker who has helped with recruiting efforts at Smith Barney's:

One response that would impress me in a job interview, if I were to ask a candidate what he or she had done with their time away from the workforce, would include an explanation about how he or she had tried to establish their own business. That shows initiative; the candidate had not remained idle. Another positive action could be taking the time off to improve him- or herself in certain things by getting, for example, business training. That again shows initiative. Finally, another interesting choice could involve fulfilling a lifetime dream. This could take the form of traveling around the world. I think such activities are healthy because they help open one's eyes and broaden one's perspective. Candidates should use periods of unemployment creatively.

How to Address Gaps in Your Work Record

After you have thought about creative ways to use your time off, you must also consider how you will address gaps in your work record when speaking to an interviewer. One useful tip: Don't sound defensive during the interview about your period of unemployment. It is best that you present that period not as a setback, but as a wonderful opportunity or pause in your career—a time you developed your skills or your ideas more. This section describes ways to respond to questions about periods of unemployment.

Specific Responses if You Were Laid Off

Keep several issues in mind when responding to questions about why you were laid off. The greatest concern your potential new employer will have is whether your termination reflected poor performance on your part. If you were a lazy or irresponsible worker, your new employer will be more hesitant to hire you. So, if you were *not* laid off because of performance issues, you should make that clear. That is, if you were laid off

---

**HOW TO ADDRESS QUESTIONS ABOUT
YOUR TERMINATION IF YOU WERE DOWNSIZED**

➤ Don't be defensive!
➤ Emphasize the benefits of what you learned at your job before you were laid off.
➤ Emphasize any good performance reviews you received.
➤ If possible, mention that you have taken the initiative during your time off to deepen your skills through courses of certifications or to conduct research into your longer-term career goals.

for economic reasons—your company needed to downsize or stream-line, for instance, and your job was cut as a result—that information can help ease the concerns of the interviewer. Therefore, if an interviewer asks about if or why you were laid off, an early aim in your discussion should be to convey that your termination was economically related, not performance based. If you have strong references or a good performance evaluation to share, you should let the interviewer know this.

If, however, you were laid off for performance-based reasons and the interviewer is aware of this, you will have to clearly articulate any infor-mation about extenuating circumstances to help address the inter-viewer's concern about whether you will perform well. For instance, if your spouse was gravely ill and you missed many days of work to tend to his or her needs, then explain this situation to the interviewer.

In both of these cases, how you present your circumstances are important. Consider Bob, who was laid off when his company decided that it needed to downsize and cut an entire department, given the financial instability of the overall company. Bob secured an interview and was asked by the interviewer, "I note that you have been out of the workforce for five months. Were you laid off?" Bob answered "Yes," in a nondefensive, confident tone, then explained:

> *My company, as you might know, began to experience a tremendous fall in revenues with the onset of the recent recession. Our executives made the difficult decision to terminate all employees in my division as part of a process of streamlining the company's product offerings. It was disappointing for all of us, but I used the opportunity to think about where I wanted to go in my career and to tool up in some useful ways by taking courses in finance at the local college. After a couple of months, I began to research companies and positions, and that's how I discovered the great opportunity your firm is offering.*

If Your Company Went Bankrupt

If you were a part of a small company that did not survive its early stages of growth and development, or part of a more established company that could not survive, the broad strategies for presenting your situation to an interviewer remain largely the same. But there are a few additional pitfalls to watch out for. For instance, I find that many employees who are coming from this situation tend to second-guess the decisions they made about their former company's strategies and financial decisions. If the company was relatively small, and these former employees exercised a strong voice in the company's direction, they often berate themselves before interviewers without recognizing it. To explain the downfall of their former company, they say things such as, "I was a key part of the company. Unfortunately, we did not formulate a coherent strategy, so when we tried to implement it, the company failed," or, "It was a small company. We did not know how to market ourselves. We were a bunch of novices who should have done more homework before launching our business."

Comments like these, while reflecting your true sentiment, will likely prove very troublesome in the interview process. How poorly an interviewer perceives such comments will depend on the situation. For instance, suppose Jill is applying for a job that requires excellent marketing skills. Obviously, if she says, "We did not know how to market ourselves. We were a bunch of novices who should have done more homework before launching our business," this explanation of the downfall of her prior company is likely to be extremely damaging. In essence, she is saying, "I don't know how to market at all, and my decisions ended in disaster." The comments will certainly have a devastating effect on the interview outcome because Jill is applying for a job in marketing.

It is much better to present any shortcoming in a more positive light, emphasizing the challenges you faced and the decisions that went right. Similarly, it is important to point out lessons you learned from the poor outcomes. To many companies, your firsthand experience of what *not* to do in a company can be as important as knowledge about what to do in order to succeed. Here is an alternative answer that Jill could have presented about why her company failed:

Our company was a very dynamic one, and I felt honored to be chosen as one of ten employees of this start-up. So many things went right: We developed a novel idea, we constructed an outstanding business plan, and we brainstormed effectively as a team to determine how best to implement our strategy. Everything was going relatively smoothly, but then we hit the rough waters of the recession.

Funding everywhere seemed to dry up as investors became much more cautious. We miscalculated how much money we would have available for our marketing campaigns, and this proved to be a notable mistake. Our otherwise sound marketing plan simply could not be implemented successfully on 40 percent of the funds we had expected to draw on. Without our planned marketing campaigns, our company did not grow our client base adequately, and soon we could not meet our financial obligations. It was a difficult and disappointing experience to close down the company, but I have learned a great deal about putting together a great business plan and developing contingency plans for what to do if funding evaporates. Unfortunately, in my former company, we did not have a contingency plan in place. But I have those valuable experiences now to draw on in my next job.

Excellent! This presentation is much more attractive to the employer. The information conveyed to the employer paints the candidate as a successful professional who took the risk and initiative to participate in a dynamic start-up. Even though the start-up failed, the candidate maintains a positive attitude and relates that she has learned valuable lessons she can draw on in the future. This turns her experience into a positive and continues to paint her as a success in spite of this one business shortcoming.

CHAPTER 8

DEMONSTRATE BUSINESS RELEVANCE IF YOU'RE A NONTRADITIONAL HIRE

In today's business world, diversity is seen as an asset. Diversity does not simply mean ethnic or cultural diversity, but also geographical and professional diversity. This chapter focuses on the interviewing candidate with a nontraditional or nonbusiness background—that is, a candidate without a background in business, economics, finance, or accounting. Recognizing the value of diverse experiences and how they can lend themselves to innovation, interviewers today are often interested in not only traditional hires, but also in candidates who have majored in public policy, engineering, medicine, computer science, and other nonbusiness fields.

Often, when nontraditional candidates fail to secure mainstream business jobs, it is not because they are nontraditional candidates, per se. More often, the reason is that they did not know how to communicate the value and relevance of their training, skills, and experiences to the interviewer in a way the interviewer could understand and value. When interviewing for a business position, you must in a minimal way be able to speak in the language of business, conveying your experiences and skills in a way that uses terms familiar to the business interviewer and that emphasizes skills relevant to the business world.

For instance, I have worked with engineers who have decided to embark on a business career, hoping to eventually blend their engineering expertise with business knowledge and run an engineering company of their own. They approach consulting companies to secure general strategic management positions that will not draw directly on their engineering expertise. When often interviewing, these engineers make the mistake of minimizing the relevance of their experience. Moreover, they often speak in terms that the interviewer has difficulty understanding and does not value. Consider Shawn, who served as an engineer at a telecommunications company for four years before trying to secure a job as a consultant at a top mainstream strategy consulting company. The interviewer asked Shawn to explain how his responsibilities in his current position as an engineering project manager were relevant to the position he was seeking as a business consultant. Shawn made a typical mistake and offered this reply:

> *Well, as a project manager, my role is to implement the information technology projects requested by our clients. I match the specifications of their systems to the products we offer, and I work with other engineers to ensure that the projects can be implemented in timely fashion. Sometimes, I find incompatibilities between the servers they use and the Internet interfaces they need to develop. Similarly, if they need to have remote access to computing services, the type of databases they use can pose problems. In much of our work, I have also found it is better to work using some of the older matrix configurations, rather than using some of the more recent derivatives. My work has not involved much business strategy work, which is why I am applying for this position at your company. I am hoping to pick up the skills that will help me to achieve my longer-term goal of running my own company.*

Ding! Most likely, Shawn would have lost the job opportunity with that answer. Many elements of this response are less than ideal. First, Shawn launches into a discussion of the technical aspects of his job, using references to interfaces and matrix configurations that the interviewer might not understand. Most likely, the interviewer is thinking, "What? I can't understand a thing Shawn is saying." The interviewer would next think, "This candidate would not be able to converse easily with a business client of ours."

Second, Shawn keeps referring to himself—"I match the specifications," "I have found it is better to work using some of the older matrix configurations," and so forth. Yet his title is project manager, which implies he is managing a project. Normally in projects, there are multiple team members. Shawn's continual reference to himself is not necessarily a hint that he does not work well in teams, but it clearly indicates that he does not understand the importance of conveying that he knows how to work in teams. In many companies today, teamwork is critical, so Shawn should be emphasizing his team leadership, using *we* and terms associated with teamwork and leadership.

Third, Shawn indicates that his skills are not relevant by stating, "My work has not involved much business strategy work." While companies may hire you with no relevant experience, most companies would like to hear you explain clearly the relevance of your experience. Let's explore how a nontraditional hire can convincingly portray the relevance of his or her experience and skills.

Transferable Skills: Making a Nontraditional Background Relevant

The concept of transferable skills is particularly important for nontraditional job seekers who must demonstrate that their education and work experience have given them skills that—though used in a totally different context before—can be used or adapted in the new environment to enable the candidate to succeed in the workplace. To demonstrate how a candidate with a nontraditional background often picks up business-relevant experiences, consider these dimensions of work experience, which provide transferable skills you might employ whether you are working in the health care industry or in a computer consulting company:

Performing analysis
Performing math computations
Problem solving
Delivering presentations

Prioritizing tasks
Participating in high-performing teams
Leading teams
Setting goals
Communicating goals
Delegating tasks
Managing work flow
Setting clear deadlines
Coaching team members
Communicating effectively with superiors
Communicating effectively with peers
Communicating effectively with clients
Developing business plans
Securing buy-in for a project
Marketing a project
Implementing change

Phrasing Matters

This list suggests types of activities and skills that an interviewing candidate might have developed during jobs in fields as diverse as engineering and public policy. To convey nonbusiness experience in relevant terms, therefore, nontraditional candidates should draw on the language of business to speak about their work, conveying in compelling terms the business relevance of their experience. Considering this, Shawn could have come up with a very different answer to the question of how his responsibilities in his current computer company position are relevant to the position he is seeking as a general business consultant who will not have special responsibility for computer clients but will serve a broader set of clients from a wide range of sectors. As he explained how his responsibilities in his computer company position are relevant to the available job, Shawn might have replied this way:

My role as a project manager at our computer company centers on leadership and on effective team management. In my projects, I manage teams of seven or eight talented individuals on complex projects designed to help our clients offer better products and services. We are the point of contact between my company and our clients, so it is key that our work goes well. We are responsible for keeping my company's client base strong and growing our business. Part of my role, of course, is technical—I match our best IT products to our clients' needs. I am able to draw on my analytical skills to ensure a great match. But more importantly, I harness the energy and talents of the team to come together and brainstorm about these issues, and together we always emerge with excellent alternatives for clients. I enjoy implementing our solutions.

I have succeeded in my position because I have mastered many of the important team management skills that bring success—such as time management, setting goals, and problem solving. I also know how to work with clients and implement solutions. I bring all of these skills with me to your company. I hope to further refine those skills while also

TIPS FOR NONTRADITIONAL CANDIDATES IN A MAINSTREAM BUSINESS INTERVIEW

➤ Avoid speaking in highly technical terms if you are not interviewing for a technical job.

➤ Communicate your skills in business-relevant terms, focusing on transferable skills.

➤ Study key business sources to learn basic business principles.

➤ Demonstrate a clear willingness to learn in new environment, and underscore adaptability.

➤ Appear versed in basic business etiquette such as how to dress and whether to take notes.

➤ Take courses or seminars when possible to learn business principles.

➤ Demonstrate a clear understanding of the industry and position you are applying for.

➤ Articulate clear and compelling reasons for changing your profession or direction.

➤ Become familiar with professionals who have made similar career changes to the one you seek to make, and cite their success as examples if appropriate.

➤ Emphasize how your uniqueness can add to the company.

learning and employing broader business principles through my new position with your company.

Showing That Your Skills and Knowledge Are Relevant: An Insider's View

In today's business world, companies value diversity and sometimes wish to hire candidates whose educational or work backgrounds differ from the typical candidate, as long as the interviewers are confident that such nontraditional candidates can make the transition into their new field. If you have a nontraditional background, what can help convince an interviewer that you will be an asset and can make a transition to a new field or new business career? Trained with a medical background, Hans transitioned to the business world and has held a managerial position with a leading-edge health care company. He has also served as director of several small companies. Many of his colleagues have MBAs from schools such as MIT and Harvard, and others come from nontraditional backgrounds. Hans shares his insights from his success as a nontraditional candidate for business jobs and from his role helping with recruiting efforts in his health care company:

I have learned from experience that there are several key steps to interviewing like a top MBA if you are someone who is coming with a nontraditional educational or work background and trying to make a transition into a new field or new career in the business world. Below are some winning steps that you can take:

- **Speak lucidly about how the company will profit from your knowledge, skills, and nontraditional experience.** Will the company gain a greater depth of knowledge in a key product area? Will it be able to relate better to a new set of clientele with you as a member of the team? Are your skills universal—team leadership, interpersonal, or problem-solving skills, for instance? Be clear about what your diverse background enables you to bring to the table that can enhance the interviewing company.

- **Use professional language.** If you are a "techie" applying to a business job, drop the tech talk. If you are a medical professional applying to a mainstream job, speak in terms the layman will understand. Don't speak in such intricate terms or in such casual terms that you will not be viewed as knowing what professional business language sounds like. Use language that both sides in the interview can understand.
- **Use key words.** Even beyond using professional language, adopt the professional language used in the industry and company to which you are applying. Understand the key buzzwords, but don't overuse them.
- **Speak in a clearly structured way.** If you deliver clear messages, that will be nothing but an asset in the interview.
- **Show that you understand what the company is looking for.** To do this, you must articulate your understanding of the job and its responsibilities and show how your skills, experience, and knowledge are useful for the available job.

These simple steps are powerful and can help you interview like a top MBA. These steps helped me transition from the medical world to a business leadership role in a global health care company. Now, when I conduct job interviews and I meet candidates with nontraditional backgrounds who put these steps to use, I become confident through the interview that the nontraditional candidate can make the transition into the business world and be a huge contributor to our company.

Conveying Your Skills and Experience as Transferable: An Insider's View

Many professionals in today's business world seek to move into new careers or leverage their knowledge and skills within nontraditional business arenas. While many employers recognize the value of diverse employment or educational backgrounds, how can nontraditional candidates convey their backgrounds in job interviews in ways that will assure an employer they can make a successful transition into a new career? Susan Himmelfarb, principal of the Himmelfarb Group, an executive recruiting company specializing in placements in the nonprofit and philanthropic sector, shares her expertise. A graduate of Harvard University, Ms. Himmelfarb has helped many professionals to interview like top MBAs, effectively presenting their nontraditional skills and knowledge.

As someone who has specialized in professional placements in not-for-profit organizations through my executive recruiting company, I know that not-for-profit boards of directors and executives recognize the value of hiring leaders with nontraditional backgrounds. In the nonprofit world, a "nontraditional" background is often considered to be any background in the private rather than the not-for-profit sector. In order to secure jobs in the not-for-profit world, private-sector professionals must show clearly how their experience can be drawn upon to bring positive outcomes to not-for-profit organizations. Just as someone with an engineering background must communicate clearly how their analytical and problem-solving skills have prepared them to be a good consultant when applying for a mainstream business consulting job, professionals moving from the private to the not-for-profit sector must also interview skillfully to convince not-for-profit boards of directors and executives that they can put their private-sector skills to effective work in the not-for-profit world. In my examples of how to do this, I will pinpoint not-for-profit examples in which private-sector individuals are seeking to enter the nonprofit world. But, these principles can be used by most professionals with nontraditional backgrounds who are seeking to change careers. Beyond conducting excellent background research on the not-for-profit to which they are applying (doing Internet and literature searches, speaking to colleagues with similar jobs, and so forth), there are specific tips that can help any candidate with a nontraditional background interview for a job in a new industry or sector.

Consider carefully the differences between the two job sectors. In the case of a private-sector professional making the transition to the not-for-profit world, a job candidate must think very carefully about the difference in the jobs they have held in the past and the new position they are seeking. It is not enough to go into an interview with the attitude that "I have excellent organizational and leadership skills from the for-profit world, so I can help your not-for-profit to improve your performance." You must be thoughtful about the differences between the private and not-for-profit sectors and be able to articulate what those differences are. A potential employer will be reassured to hear you acknowledge that there are differences and clearly state how you will deal with those differences and your new environment.

Be able to articulate how your skills and experience translate. As you approach the job interview, you must be able to show that you have a firm understanding of the key responsibilities of the job you are seeking, of the tasks that you must complete excellently in order to uphold your responsibilities, and of the skills needed to complete the tasks well. You can't simply issue a blanket statement that you will be able to handle the responsibilities of the job. You must be able to pinpoint for the interviewer the specific skills/tasks of the job and highlight where you have previously demonstrated those skills and when you have completed similar tasks. For example, if the not-for-profit job you are seeking will require you to form a new division of the organization, you should be able to cite instances in which you created a new team and built management and organizational processes in your prior jobs, and relate that to the responsibilities of the not-for-profit job you are seeking. Similarly, if the not-for-profit you are applying to needs new strategic direction, your job during the interview is to cite specific examples about when you have demonstrated strategic leadership in your past employment. The interviewers may not make those links themselves, so you must do that for them.

Acknowledge the new skills you must develop. In most cases, when a nontraditional candidate is seeking to move into a new career area, there will be some skills required by the new job that the candidate may not have. It is best if you acknowledge those needed skills and provide reasons why you are confident you will be able to quickly and effectively develop those skills. Suggesting a plan for how you will do so can also help alleviate a potential employer's concerns about your ability to make the transition.

Take steps to fill the gaps, if possible. If you are making a transition to a new career, once you identify the skills you will need that you do not already have, you should try to build those skills before the interview if possible. For example, if you need good managerial skills but have only a couple of years of managerial experience and feel you need more for a potential new job, take a course in that area and be able to speak about how this has complemented and supplemented your knowledge. Of course, doing this requires planning ahead and assumes you have months to devote to developing needed skills.

Use the language of the new organization or field. Don't use language specific to your current job or industry in an interview. Industry or job-specific language is simply jargon to anyone outside of that world. At best, it creates a distance between you and your interviewer. At worst, you will just not be understood. Take the time to translate the words and terms of your former field or sector into commonly understood language or into the professional terminology of the industry or job you are targeting.

There are several mistakes to avoid as well:

Don't overestimate the ease of the new job. In my work in the not-for-profit world, when I see private-sector candidates approach potential not-for-profit jobs, they sometimes make the mistake of conveying the impression that, given their private-industry experience, any work in the not-for-profit world will be easy. This can come across as arrogance. It is self-defeating, and it also shows a lack of understanding of challenges in the not-for-profit world. Acknowledge the challenges of the new job, outline instances when you have faced similar challenges in your past experience, and explain clearly to the interviewer how these relate.

Don't assume that you don't need to explain clearly your past level of responsibilities. Another problem I see with candidates making the transition between career types is sometimes they consider their past experience so much more valuable than experience in the new field that when going into the interview for their potential new job, they make no effort to clearly explain the scope of managerial or leadership roles. Be careful to explain what level of responsibility you have held in the past and how that has prepared you for both your potential new job and your potential new environment.

Avoid exaggerating. In an effort to make your experience more relevant, don't exaggerate the level of your former responsibilities. Learn something about how the level of organizational responsibility and complexity at which you've worked compares with that of the position you're seeking. It may seem to you that your previous work was at a level of responsibility analogous to the level of the position you're interviewing for. But be sure to confirm that, to avoid appearing as if you don't understand and appreciate the differences, if they exist, and the greater demands they might place on you if you were to be hired for the position.

Avoid parroting information back. Because you are trying to make a transition into a new career, you may have read up on the new organization or the new field. In the interview, avoid simply repeating information you have read on the new organization's website. Your comments about the new field and organization you are trying to join should make it clear that you have learned something about the organization. But your comments should also show that you've taken the time to bring some of your own thoughts and experiences to your thinking about the position.

If you put these practices to use, you will make your task of transitioning into a new career field much easier. One example of when I saw a nontraditional candidate make a transition excellently occurred when a very dynamic private-sector professional was seeking to move from editing and reporting to philanthropy. On its face, you might think there was little relation between her career and experience and making decisions about which grants a foundation should make. This candidate, however, in approaching my firm to be placed in this foundation job, concisely summarized the skills that would be required—analysis, research, exploring new ideas, deciding which new ideas had promise and should be pursued, thinking strategically, and writing. She made the link between those skills and the ones she had acquired working in the media. She made the links clearly and instantly in the first few minutes of our first conversation, pointing out that grant making was about setting strategy, serving as a gatekeeper, and also going after promising ideas. Within three sentences she made those connections in a way that I knew an employer would understand. As I expected, she successfully made the case to the prospective employer.

Another example of a successful transition occurred when a not-for-profit organization needed a new executive director to bring effective leadership, new visibility, and strategic direction to their organization. A private-sector individual with senior-level banking experience was selected for the position. During his interviews, this candidate described exceedingly well the strategic leadership role he had played in his firm, how he had brought new leadership to his company, and how his effective leadership had enabled him to successfully implement his strategy. He articulated these points not only in his interviews but also in his cover letter and résumé, using language that was appropriate for the new field he was seeking to enter. He also had some volunteer not-for-profit experience in his background that helped him understand and talk intelligently about making this transition.

To interview like a top MBA as you try to transition from a nontraditional background to a new career field, keep these tips in mind.

Social Science Majors Applying for a Business Job

Just as a computer specialist and an engineer are able to convey their experience in business-relevant terms, an interviewing candidate from a social science background such as public policy or political science also can do so. Consider the example of Melanie, who majored in political science and worked for two years in a government position focused on health care policy. When asked to explain the relevance of her experience to a business consulting job, she might offer this reply:

I have greatly enjoyed political science and my government job, because both enabled me to become immersed in new ideas and innovative thinking, and both presented me with opportunities to challenge exist-ing policies with new ways of approaching long-standing problems. In my job, for instance, I am able to draw on the wonderful analytical skills I developed during my political science education, when I learned how to disaggregate problems and focus on the key issues that were cre-ating a problem. A large part of my job involved completing relevant research and prioritizing the issues, and making presentations to my superiors in accessible language that laid forth the heart of the issues, and focused on the key factors to be addressed in order to improve the problem. I became a wonderful communicator, and I mastered the art of using visual aids to facilitate understanding of issues at hand. I also became excellent at persuading others through structured and clear reasoning. Once my analysis and recommendations were considered and accepted, my job was to develop an implementation plan, priori-tize the next steps, and lead a team to implement the new policies. All of those skills and experiences will enable me to be a great consultant for your company.

END YOUR INTERVIEW EXCELLENTLY

Generally when an interview comes to a conclusion, the interviewer often asks one of three questions: whether you have anything else you'd like to discuss about your record, whether you have questions, or what you will do if you do not secure the job. Your goal in the interview is to secure a job offer, so you should approach each end-of-the-interview question with that goal in mind. This chapter presents some ideas about good ways to address each of these three questions.

End-of-Interview Chance to Discuss Your Record

Often, in bringing an interview to a conclusion, the interviewer asks you whether there is anything else you'd like to discuss about your record. Many of the ways you can approach this opportunity will enable you to take advantage of this chance to end the interview with a lasting, positive impression. You should use this question as an opportunity to emphasize your winning attributes, relevant skills, and record of success. In doing this, consider the attributes and qualifications you outlined in Chapter 3 as the key ones desired in the ideal candidate for the available job. Think of the attributes and qualifications you highlighted as the ones you would like to focus on in the interview to demonstrate a match. When given an opportunity at the end of an interview to discuss your record, focus your response on those winning attributes and qualifications.

Recap Your Winning Themes

You can take the opportunity to recap the themes you had hoped to present during the interview. Since this is the close of the interview, you should not elaborate for too long. Concisely recap a summary of the skills and attributes you bring to the company and restate your deep interest in the company. For instance, when Lindsay concluded her interview with a strategic consulting firm, she responded with these words:

> *I thank you again for meeting with me and discussing your firm with me. As I mentioned, since college I have been working toward a position like this. I have devoted a great deal of effort to developing a strong skill set in marketing, business strategy, and finance through a consulting firm that specializes in start-ups. Now is an ideal time for me to move to a larger firm with a more diversified client base. With my leadership successes, I believe I can help to grow your new division. I hope to have the opportunity to join your firm.*

This answer provides a brief recap of the candidate's main theme: that she has a strong skill set and leadership successes that can serve as the basis for excellent outcomes in her new position. The positive attitude and confidence of the candidate's response, combined with a restatement of the candidate's themes, will leave a positive impression.

What to Ask the Interviewer

Instead of asking if you have anything to add, some interviewers close an interview by asking you to pose questions to him or her. This is a great opportunity to demonstrate your knowledge about the company or industry, underscore your deep interest in the company, and further demonstrate that your qualifications and attributes are a good fit for the available job.

While the chance to ask questions at the end of an interview is a wonderful opportunity, err on the side of caution. In your initial interviews with a company, your goal is to land an offer, so you do not want to ask risky or highly sensitive questions at this time. Pointed questions aimed at probing to see if there is a misfit between you and the company are generally best saved for later, after you have secured an offer and are trying to determine whether you should accept it.

Questions to Avoid

In general, when thinking about which questions to ask, it is useful to know which ones you should *avoid*:

1. Avoid questions that paint you in a bad light, such as deep concerns about salary levels. Questions such as "I hear your professionals get little sleep—is that rumor true?" or "I wanted to make sure your compensation matches what I am currently making. What salary are you proposing?" can cause a negative reaction from an interviewer. The former question might make you seem as if you have an aversion to hard work or as if you will not fit into a prevailing work culture, and the latter may make you appear too focused on money. Questions of this nature are best rephrased more softly and asked after the job has been offered to you.

2. Avoid questions that demonstrate a lack of fit between the company and you. For instance if the corporate work in your interviewing company is completed primarily in teams, avoid saying, "I prefer to work individually, so I would like to know if the majority of work here is done in teams." If you know that work is done mostly individually, then this question may not be so horrible. However, if the corporate work is completed mostly in teams, you have just demonstrated a misfit between you and the company. On this basis alone, you might have jeopardized your chance of securing a job offer.

3. Avoid asking questions that are personal, such as, "I am concerned about what happens in three years if I want to have children, because I was recently married. Do you have children, and how have you worked this in with your work life here?" This question is one you might ask after you have secured a job offer or if you are in the midst of a callback interview and are trying to determine whether you

really want this job. In a first or early-stage interview, an interviewer may consider this too personal and may form a negative impression of you as a result.

4. Avoid asking questions that are controversial. Try to stay away from sensitive issues when you are trying to secure a job offer.

5. Avoid asking questions that indicate you have not done your homework about the job, company, or industry. For example, if you ask, "What does your consulting company focus on?" the interviewer will think that you could have found an answer by reading the company website or annual report. Your aim is to sound informed, prepared, and interested in the job. Try to avoid sounding as if you have put little effort into exploring the job responsibilities, company, or industry before coming to the interview.

What *Not* to Do if Offered a Chance to Ask Questions: An Insider's View

Celeste Garcia, formerly of PricewaterhouseCoopers and currently managing director of consulting services for Ivy Planning Group, LLC, offers advice about what not to say if the interviewer invites you to ask questions:

Don't ask about benefits early on before you get an offer. That would make me, the interviewer, nervous and suggest that you are more focused on your needs than your possible contribution to the organization.

Equally important, the skilled interviewee never chooses not to ask a question at all. In order to interview like a top MBA, you should *always* have questions to ask. This demonstrates that you are interested in what the interviewer has to say, as well as very interested in the job. Even when you have posed all of your chosen questions to other interviewers in my company, I would not know that, so ask me the same ones! You might get a different answer.

Questions to Ask

Now that you know what to avoid, let's explore best practices of how to use end-of-the-interview questions well. If the interviewer asks you to pose questions, stay with simple questions that have fairly predictable answers. As much as possible, ask questions that help demonstrate a fit between you and the company. Also ask knowledgeable questions to demonstrate you have done your homework about the job, company, or industry. Here is an example:

> *I was interested to learn when reading through current business articles that, given your corporate culture that encourages innovation, your company has doubled its client base and is seeking to grow its Houston base in the area of gas and energy consulting. What have you most enjoyed about the work in this area?*

Through this question, the candidate conveys to the interviewer that he is familiar with the direction the company is taking. The question also asks the interviewer to comment about his or her own experience at the company, which will likely create a positive reaction.

In posing questions to the interviewer, avoid sounding as if you do not know the basics about the company or industry, or as if you have not completed your homework about the job offered. Here are some sample questions that you might want to consider when thinking about what to ask your interviewer at the end of an interview:

- What have you most enjoyed about working for this company?
- How is your company seeking to grow?
- How is this division seeking to grow?
- How would you describe your firm's culture?
- What are the most important divisional goals at this time?
- What are the most important corporate goals at this time?
- What makes this company particularly good at what it does?
- How does the work of this department fit with the overall goals of the company?
- What do you foresee as the biggest changes to your service or product lines in the future?
- Who do the leaders of this department report to?
- What have you most enjoyed about this atmosphere?
- Where does the company see itself in five years?

Demonstrating Knowledge While Asking Questions

If you would really like to impress the interviewer, you might consider introducing a question from this list with a brief sentence or two to demonstrate your knowledge of the job, company, or industry. For instance, rather than simply asking, "How is your company seeking to grow?" you might choose to ask the question this way:

> *Having read a great deal about this industry and the growth of the health care sector within it, I was interested to learn that recently your company has expanded mostly through its health care consulting work and its restructuring consulting work. Looking forward, how else is your company seeking to grow?*

What I Like to Hear at the End of the Interview: An Insider's View

Wilson Shelbon, a former manager at Procter & Gamble gives end-of-the-interview advice:

When interviewing candidates from top schools, certain end-of-the-interview behavior makes me think of some candidates as good interviewees. For instance, when given a chance to ask questions, the candidate should ask more questions concerning the scope and prospects of the position. That shows enthusiasm. But be sure to structure your questions in ways that clarify you have a solid understanding of the scope and prospects to begin with. That way, you will show both enthusiasm and competence.

Explaining What You'll Do if Not Offered the Position

A third common variation for how interviewers close an interview involves questions about your future plans. Interviewers have different ways of asking what you will do if you are not offered the position for which you are interviewing. The interviewer might not ask you that precise question but might catch you off guard by asking where else you are interviewing. If an interviewer asks this directly, be straightforward about where else you are scheduled to interview or where you have recently interviewed. Integrity is very important in the business world, so you do not want to do anything that would call your integrity into question, such as not telling the truth about where you are interviewing. Recruiters at companies in the same industry often know each other, so you do not want to seem less than forthcoming and have your interviewer discover later that you omitted information or fudged your answers.

Consider Cindy, who applied for employment as a dental assistant for a large office. If asked where else she is interviewing, she could answer as follows:

I have applied at the top three dental practices in this area. However, your company is my top choice. As I mentioned, I have been looking for a company that is known for focusing on providing affordable dental care with excellent health care staff. The way your practice is structured and your specialization, in combination with the corporate culture of your company, makes your dental practice very appealing to me.

This response does a good job of answering the question in a straightforward manner but also underscores why this particular company is a good fit for the candidate.

Another version of this query is more straightforward. The interviewer might state, "Well, you are an interesting candidate, but we are not certain about hiring you at this time. What will you do if you are not offered a position here?" In many ways, you can interpret this question as "where else are you interviewing?" Explain that you have or are currently exploring alternatives, but underscore that their job is ideal for you. Cindy might choose to respond in this way:

I would be disappointed if I did not secure this job, of course, because I sense such a fit between my qualifications and goals and the culture of your dental practice. However, I am not one to give up quickly. If I do

not secure this job, I will think about how to strengthen my candidacy
and take steps toward doing so. At the same time, I will consider other
opportunities in this general career field, because I am certain that
becoming a dental assistant is what I wish to do.

This response is upbeat and underscores the fact that Cindy intends to
work in this area and will not give up on her goals prematurely. This
response also indicates that Cindy seeks to continually strengthen her
skills and is forward-looking—attributes that the interviewer will likely
find appealing.

Now that you understand how to respond to three common ways in
which interviews come to a close, Chapter 10 will explore other ways
to ensure you reinforce a positive, lasting impression.

CHAPTER 10

FOLLOW UP, REINFORCING A POSITIVE, LASTING IMPRESSION

It is important that you end your interview well, reinforcing a positive, lasting impression. Chapter 9 elaborated on ways to do that. But many candidates who interview for jobs are uncertain how to follow up an interview. If they wish to write a letter of appreciation, they are often uncertain *to whom* to write, *when* to write, and *what* to write. For instance, if there are two rounds of interviews, it is sometimes unclear whether writing follow-up or thank-you letters after the first round of interviews will appear too aggressive or even manipulative. This chapter discusses some best practices for following up an interview.

What to Do After the Interview: An Insider's View

Byron, former consultant at Booz Allen Hamilton and McKinsey & Company, offers this advice about following up:

After the interview, remind the interviewer who you are by writing a brief note—even if it is just a brief e-mail—that makes reference to some of the things you spoke about with the interviewer. Express your appreciation for their time, and mention that you greatly enjoyed getting to meet them. I have received many responses from interviewers letting me know they really appreciated it when I sent them notes after the interview. It adds a nice touch.

How to Follow Up if Another Interview Might Follow

When you have interviewed for a job, regardless of whether further interviewing might take place, it is a good idea to send a follow-up letter within forty-eight hours after your initial interview, if possible. Follow-up letters are excellent for multiple reasons. First, they enable you to keep your image and candidacy in the interviewer's mind. A letter also personalizes the interaction you had with the interviewer and can make the interviewer feel appreciated. If the interviewer feels good about the interaction with you, you are more likely to have a positive outcome. In addition, writing a follow-up letter is an excellent sign of professionalism and courtesy, which will reflect positively on your sense of business etiquette.

When writing this follow-up letter, you should address the letter to the main person who interviewed you. For instance, if you interviewed with eight professionals in a firm on one day, write to the main interviewer or the human resources manager who was your point of contact for the interviews. It is usually not advisable to write to each individual you interviewed with; that can be misinterpreted as too pushy or too aggressive. Rather, your letter might simply request that the main interviewer pass on your sentiment to all other people who interviewed you.

The best content in an instance when the interviewing process may not yet be complete is content that focuses on accomplishing four tasks: It should express your appreciation for the opportunity to meet with representatives of the company. It should express your deep interest in the job. It should emphasize how your positive impression of the company was reinforced through your discussions with the talented representatives/professionals with whom you met. And it should speak enthusiastically about the possibility of joining the company. The following letter accomplishes those tasks:

Dear Ms. Flores:

I wanted to thank you for taking the time to meet with me yesterday about the job you are offering in the Marketing Department. It was a pleasure to have the opportunity to introduce myself and to meet the many talented professionals of your company. Having completed detailed research about your company, its culture, and its plans, I entered the interviewing process very excited to meet key personnel and discuss the possibility of joining your team. The highly positive image I had of your company was only deepened and reinforced by the dynamic team members I met throughout the day yesterday. I find the ideas you are pushing forward and the goals of the Marketing Department to be very impressive, and I believe that with my leadership skills and record of marketing success, I can be a very valuable addition to the team. My interest in the position remains strong, and I hope to be able to add my creativity and demonstrated leadership abilities to your marketing efforts.

Thank you so much for your time.

With much appreciation,

James Cohen

How to Follow Up if the Company Gives You an Offer

If the company has already offered you a job, after you decide whether to join the company, you should write a letter to each person who interviewed you. If you have chosen to accept the position, writing a letter soon thereafter lays the groundwork for positive interactions after you join the firm. If you have chosen not to join the firm, the letter still creates a foundation for positive interactions, because the recipients will appreciate that you took the time to express your appreciation for meeting with them. If you ever seek to join the firm at a later date, you will have helped solidify a lasting, positive impression.

For instance, if you decide to accept the offer, you might write a note informing each person who interviewed you and thanking each of them for taking the time to do so. Try to personalize each letter. Refer to your notes for bits of information you might want to refer to, and in addition to more job-centered topics, refer to more jovial topics that you might have spoken about. For instance, after accepting an offer following her interview, Kendra wrote the following letter to a vice president who had interviewed her:

Dear Ms. Mendez:

Thank you so much for meeting with me last week to discuss the managerial position that is available in the business division of your company. I greatly enjoyed speaking to you at length and hearing about your experiences in the firm. I particularly appreciated your candor as you spoke about the key differences between your firm and its main rivals. I have decided to accept the offer that your company has extended to me, and I will be joining the team in two months. I am very excited about this opportunity and this wonderful transition in my career. I will look forward to many interactions with you in the coming months.

With my best wishes,

Kendra Reynolds

How to Follow Up if the Company Chooses Not to Hire You

In the unfortunate instance when the company decides not to make you an offer, consider writing a letter to the main person who interviewed you. Writing a letter soon after you receive the decision lays the groundwork for future positive interactions if you ever interview with the firm again. It will help you leave a positive impression. Even if you never join the firm, professionals within the same industry often encounter each other, and your letter may help lay the groundwork for future collaboration or friendly relations that might serve an important business purpose in the future.

Following a rejection for a job, Bob Johnson chose to write this polite letter to the main interviewer:

Dear Ms. Eckstein:

I recently received your letter informing me that I was not selected for the position as assistant manager of your health care division. Nonetheless, I wanted to sincerely thank you and the rest of the health care senior staff with whom I met, for taking the time to let me introduce myself and to learn more about your company. I was very impressed by your company and your dynamic staff, and I remain very interested in your company. If the opportunity ever arises for me to join your team, please be in touch.

Thank you for your time and consideration. I hope our paths will cross in future business dealings.

Sincerely,

Bob Johnson

Generally you will write only one letter to the main interviewer. But if you happened to strike up a particularly strong rapport with any other interviewer, you might consider also sending a brief note to that person. But use caution. People often feel uncomfortable if they feel they have rejected you, so if you write a letter to anyone aside from the main interviewer, keep the letter brief and upbeat. Refer to your notes for bits of information you might want to mention in order to personalize the letter, weaving in references to lighter or more jovial topics that you might have spoken about with that interviewer. Following that same rejection for a job, Bob Johnson wrote the following note to another interviewer with whom he had struck up a particularly vibrant conversation:

Dear Mr. Mason,

I received news two days ago that I was not chosen for the position as assistant manager of your health care division. I was disappointed that I will not have the opportunity to join your team. But I wanted to express my deep gratitude that you took the time to speak with me about your company, career opportunities, and the future of the health care industry. In the future also, I will try to remember to avoid the orange bicycles on the pathway that you warned me about near our home!

Thank you for your time and consideration. I hope our paths will cross in future business dealings.

Sincerely,

Bob Johnson

Conclusion

Chapters 1 through 10 have introduced you to best practices that can help you deliver an outstanding interview. These principles outline ways to avoid the "top ten interview mistakes" mentioned in Chapter 1. Keep these best practices in mind during every job interview. Here's a quick recap:

Top Ten Interview Dos
1. Create a great first impression.
2. Do your homework about the company, industry, job offered, and interviewer.
3. Use your résumé as an effective interviewing tool.
4. Demonstrate a fit through your responses to key questions.
5. Shape the interview.
6. Address concerns about clear weaknesses effectively.
7. Explain any periods of unemployment well.
8. Demonstrate the business relevance of your experience and education (if you are a nontraditional candidate).
9. End your interview excellently with wonderful closing comments or well-considered questions.
10. Follow up your interview so as to reinforce a lasting, positive impression.

Above all, practice your delivery. Practice can make your delivery much smoother, so rehearse. To aid your effort, in Part II we provide 100 questions and sample answers to help you think about your own responses to common interview questions.

PART II

100 TOUGH QUESTIONS AND HOW TO ANSWER THEM

GENERAL RÉSUMÉ QUESTIONS

1. Take me through your résumé, starting with your first full-time job. (Or, "Describe your career progression to date.")

What They Are Looking For: This question gives you an opportunity to convey your key skills, responsibilities, and achievements. You should use this question strategically, carving your answer in a way that emphasizes the skills the employer will most value. Use your time strategically. Do not dwell long on parts of your work career that had fewer significant responsibilities or major accomplishments. Spend more time on the aspects of your work experience that highlight your key characteristics such as leadership, team management, and excellent analytical skills. As you proceed with a summary of your work experience, emphasize an expanding set of responsibilities, any promotions you received, and your deepening skill set.

Sample Answer: "After I majored in computer science, I sought a job that would enable me to use the analytical skills I had developed. I landed a wonderful position at a Fortune 500 company, and in my first job as an analyst, I learned to combine my computing expertise with strategy principles. I excelled and was then promoted to associate, where my responsibilities expanded to include aspects of project management.

In my current position as an associate, I have also developed financial analysis skills."

Analysis of Answer: This answer is good because it presents a progression of skills and implies the job candidate has continually excelled in his or her job.

What to Avoid: Avoid speaking only about the tasks you completed, rather than the skills you garnered. A good answer often blends information about both skills and tasks.

2. Describe the job you had before your present one.

What They Are Looking For: The interviewer is interested in hearing whether you can present a concise, structured answer while also transmitting valued information about your skills and capabilities. Because the interviewer is asking you about the job before your current one, you have the opportunity to talk about the activities and achievements that enabled you to move on to your current, and hopefully more advanced, job.

Sample Answer: "In my prior job, my work included three main areas of responsibility. First, I was in charge of managing a team of five junior team members in completing a significant project for one of my company's core clients. This included setting goals for the team and assigning the specific roles and tasks of each team member. I also had to manage their work to ensure we were making headway toward our goals. Second, I was responsible for managing the company's relationship with that core client. This meant nurturing the relationship with them by meeting with representatives and ensuring that our work was addressing their needs. Finally, I served as a liaison between the team and my superiors, so that my superiors understood how things were progressing and could continue to keep an eye on how they hoped our relationship with this client would develop."

Analysis of Answer: This answer was structured, concise, and to the point, and it presents a clear range of responsibilities.

What to Avoid: Avoid speaking only about the tasks you completed, rather than the skills you garnered. A good answer often blends information about both skills and tasks.

3. **Tell me about what level of responsibility you have in your current job.**

What They Are Looking For: The interviewer is interested in hearing whether you can present a concise, structured answer while also conveying valued information about your skills and capabilities. Your answer to this question is particularly important because, as you answer about your responsibilities and your roles in your current job, you will also be conveying to the interviewer information about whether your experience range and skills make you qualified to handle the responsibilities of the job the company is trying to fill. Take advantage of this opportunity to speak clearly about your achievements and skills and about how your successes have encouraged your superiors to entrust you with increasing levels of responsibility. Also take the time to mention any instances where you made unique or innovative contributions to your work environment. Initiative and leadership are highly valued.

Sample Answer: "I feel honored to be in my current position because I was promoted after only five months in my prior job, given my strong performance. In my current role, I have an expanded set of responsibilities, which include not only managing my team on critical projects that help bring in about 20 percent of the firm's revenue, but also helping to maintain strong client relations. This latter responsibility includes meeting with our clients' representatives and keeping an effective dialogue there. I must also be creative about organizing get-togethers between our clients' and our company's representatives. Another key area that has been added to my responsibilities is to help grow our client base, which means marketing our services to potential new clients."

Analysis of Answer: This answer is structured and presents a clear range of responsibilities. The job candidate does a good job of weaving in extra information about helping to bring in 20 percent of the company's revenues and about receiving a quick promotion. This is a good use of the opportunity presented by the question.

What to Avoid: Avoid sounding as if your level of responsibility has not prepared you for the job for which you are interviewing.

4. Describe the role you played on your most recent project.

What They Are Looking For: As with Question 3, the interviewer is interested in hearing a structured, compelling answer that relays the responsibilities and skills you employ in your current job. Your answer to this question is particularly important because you will be conveying to the interviewer information about whether you have the skills and experience needed to excel in the position the company is trying to fill. Touch on the most important aspects of your role that are relevant to the job you are interviewing for. For more advanced positions, the sorts of responsibilities you might speak about include teamwork, team leadership, client management, business strategy, and business development.

Sample Answer: "I served as a key team member on a team of fifteen, which was assigned responsibility for implementing a new IT system for a small business with great growth potential. My company was seeking to make inroads in the small-business market, so our success here was key. I helped to set the goals for the team—both long-term and short-term goals. I took on the task of designing the specifics of the IT system and matching it to the client's current technology programs. I played a part in meeting with the client's executives to ensure my program design would work well for them. I also guided client representatives through key discussion points in meetings. Because I delivered excellent work on time and helped other team members when they experienced difficulties, the project was a success."

Analysis of Answer: This answer is creative. Even though the candidate held a position only as a team member and not as a team leader, the candidate projected an image that made it clear that she served as an integral part of the team and that her work was important to the team's success.

What to Avoid: Even if you did not hold a leadership position, don't downplay the importance of your work. If you were an active part of a team, then you were an active part of the team's success also, so be sure to present your work that way.

5. How did you like your last job?

What They Are Looking For: The interviewer is giving you a chance to shape the discussion but still wants you to convey information that demonstrates you are a good choice for the job. This question can be considered open-ended, so you have considerable scope to steer your answer in many different directions. Take advantage. The interviewer is leaving the field wide open for a response. A response that blends references to your winning attributes with descriptions of impressive responsibilities and roles you had in your last job is likely to produce a good answer to this question.

Sample Answer: "There were so many aspects of my last job that were enjoyable. I am someone who loves a challenge, loves working in a team, and loves to solve complex problems. My last job gave me all three elements. Most of our work was built around teams. We had to work on marketing issues that were complex given the downturn in the economy and the dip in consumer spending. We had to design ways to entice reluctant buyers to purchase our goods. I enjoyed the challenge of coming up with creative ideas. My role involved harnessing the ideas of my team members and molding them into a coherent, winning combination. I hope to find these sorts of characteristics in my new work, but I am also looking to expand my role in a new position with more leadership responsibilities."

Analysis of Answer: This answer is positive, which is great. The job candidate comes across as someone with a desirable work attitude who would make a good colleague. The candidate uses this question as an opportunity to display qualities that are attractive to most job interviewers, as well as to define how he hopes to develop his skills in future work.

What to Avoid: Try to avoid sounding overly negative about your prior job if you disliked many elements about it. Start off mentioning the positives, even if you must eventually elaborate on the negative aspects of your prior job.

6. What did you like least about your last job?

What They Are Looking For: This can be considered an open-ended question, but the interviewer is still seeking information from you that will help to convince him or her that you are the right person for the advertised job. Take advantage of the open-ended nature of the question. The interviewer has left the field wide open for you to paint a picture of yourself with references to your winning attributes. But be careful. Because the interviewer is asking you to speak negatively about your last job, you should make sure not to be too negative about the job. You do not want to come across as whining. Rather, adopt an even tone, make note of the shortcomings of the job, and speak in positive terms about what you are now seeking in a job. That is, make it clear you are seeking the new job for positive reasons, not simply fleeing from a job you dislike.

Sample Answer: "What I liked the least about my last job was the resistance my team sometimes encountered from our company's executives to novel ideas. This has to be considered alongside the fact that there were so many aspects of my last job that I enjoyed. I love a challenge, working in a team, and solving complex problems. My last job gave me all of these elements. We had to work in teams on human resource issues that were complex given the downturn in the economy and the dip in our company's revenues. We did not want to fire employees, but to make ends meet, we had to adjust incomes and benefits so as to weather the difficult economy. I enjoyed the challenge of coming up with creative ideas. It was hard, though, to sell those ideas at times to a couple of upper-management members who held firm to old ideas about human resource management. After several presentations, however, we eventually persuaded them to accept many elements of our new ideas, which enabled us to implement some successful programs."

Analysis of Answer: This answer responds to the question, highlighting a negative aspect of the job briefly. But the response then quickly injects a positive tone. The job candidate comes across as someone with a positive and desirable work attitude who would make a good colleague. The candidate uses this question as an opportunity to illustrate qualities that are attractive to most job interviewers, as well as to define how she hopes to develop her skills in the future. The positive aspects of the response pave the way for the respondent to speak about the negatives without sounding sour or whining.

What to Avoid: Try to avoid sounding as if you are sour, whining, or prone to complaining a great deal.

7. Compare and contrast your experience at your last two jobs.

What They Are Looking For: This sort of question is very specific and challenging, as it asks you to quickly summarize two jobs and use clear analytical skills and language to draw comparisons and contrasts between the two positions. Most interviewers who ask this question are seeking to assess the strength of your analytical skills—how quickly you can draw out the similarities and differences of two situations. Ideally, if you followed the advice in Chapter 3, you will have made notes about each of the jobs listed on your résumé, and you will already have in the forefront of your mind the key responsibilities, achievements, and skills associated with each job. If this is the case, you will be able to more easily respond to this question.

Sample Answer: "In my job as a paralegal, my responsibilities included support for the top lawyers of our firm. I was responsible for completing key research, helping to define legal precedents, and reviewing some legal documents for consistency. What I lacked in this particular job was hands-on work with clients. I sought that in my next position, as I wanted to refine the 'people skills' that I believe are key to my future professional success. When I received an opportunity to be a legislative manager with a congressman, therefore, this represented an ideal chance. My role there included key research and definition of policy stances, but it also involved a great deal of interaction in public settings, during which I explained policy positions to citizens. While my position as a legislative manager required that I spend less time with the process of researching precedents and comparing legislation, I greatly enjoyed the expansion of my role in the area of education and communication with citizens."

Analysis of Answer: The answer does a good job of projecting the candidate as someone who is purposefully amassing a strong skill set and moving toward a longer-term goal.

What to Avoid: Avoid appearing as if you do not know how to quickly summarize the key responsibilities of each job you have held or the skills you employed in each job. If possible, also avoid appearing as if your jobs are randomly chosen and not directed toward some broader purpose.

8. Tell me about your management experience.

What They Are Looking For: Given the general nature of this question, this question falls into the category of open-ended questions. The interviewer has given you a tremendous opportunity to choose which of your management experiences you will focus on the most. As always, the interviewer wants you to relay relevant information that demonstrates your fit for the advertised job. You should use this chance to focus immediately on the winning accomplishments and responsibilities you outlined after completing the exercises of Chapter 3. You should provide a response that refers to your winning attributes, the number of promotions you have received, and any award you might have won for high performance. You also have the latitude to spend the most time on the aspects of your managerial experience that will be most valued by the employer interviewing you.

Sample Answer: "I was promoted to the position of manager after three successful years as assistant manager. In my role as manager, I oversee ten direct reports, who form three teams in our core group. My responsibilities include helping to set direction for my subordinates, reviewing their work, and providing feedback. I particularly enjoy this work because I have a good opportunity to mentor my professional staff and to help develop in them the attributes that make for successful managers, such as goal setting, communication skills, and coaching abilities."

Analysis of Answer: This answer could have been longer, but for a brief response, it achieves the important objective of transmitting information about relevant skills. This candidate clearly communicates the skills he or she employs as a manager, and these skills will be seen as transferable and relevant to any managerial position.

What to Avoid: Avoid elaborating on skills or experiences that have little or no relevance to the job for which you are interviewing.

9. Tell me about your client management experiences.

What They Are Looking For: The interviewer is looking for you to elaborate on relevant experiences, not just on any experiences. Like Question 8, this question is relatively general and falls into the category of open-ended questions. That is, the interviewer has given you a tremendous opportunity to choose which of your client management experiences to focus on the most. You should try to mention a good range of skills, if appropriate, such as your experience in meeting with clients in small-group sessions or one to one, making presentations to clients, receiving feedback from clients, or managing client work in a timely fashion. Select the elements you stress based in part on the responsibilities you are likely to have in the job for which you are interviewing.

Sample Answer: "When I was promoted to the position of manager, one of the things I most looked forward to was the increase in direct client contact. Now I have responsibility not only to manage our clients and strengthen our client relationships, but also to help our company to secure new clients. I have successfully helped to increase our client base by 20 percent, in part through referral clients. But equally importantly, I have helped to improve client relations, which has led to more business per client. I have done this by meeting more frequently with our clients to ensure our products are meeting their needs and by responding to feedback from clients. All of these skills and experiences are ones I hope to draw on as I work with your company."

Analysis of Answer: This answer achieved the important objective of transmitting information about skills and experiences that are relevant to the advertised job. This candidate clearly communicates the skills she employed in managing client relationships, and these skills will be seen as transferable.

What to Avoid: Avoid speaking at length about skills or experiences that have no relevance to the job for which you are interviewing.

QUESTIONS ABOUT CAREER GOALS

10. What are your short-term goals?

What They Are Looking For: In this question, the interviewer is seeking to see if your goals match the opportunities presented in the job for which you are interviewing. Tailor your answer in a way that answers yes to that query.

Sample Answer: "In the short term, I hope to help manage a large project that is aiming to expand social services into underserved educational institutions. In college, I was fortunate to take a number of courses about the history of such programs and about contemporary trends in that area. It is a meaningful area, and I believe that with the organizational skills I have developed through my internships, along with my education, I will bring many skills and creative ideas to a project like that. When I heard about the project your organization has begun, it sounded like a wonderful fit with my interests and skills."

Analysis of Answer: The candidate conveys a short-term goal that is compatible with the organization's interests. The candidate also explains how his education and work experience are relevant to the job.

What to Avoid: Avoid presenting a short-term goal that is not compatible with the needs or interests of the company with which you are interviewing.

11. What are your long-term goals?

What They Are Looking For: In this question, the interviewer is seeking to assess whether your goals match the opportunities presented in the available job and the company or organization offering that job. You should know the company and the position well enough to understand whether the interviewer might be bothered if you imply you do not intend to stay at the organization for the long term.

Sample Answer: "My long-term goal is to serve as the head of a retail store in a major Fortune 500 retail company. This is why I am highly interested in working for your company. Over the past few years, I have been preparing for this goal by studying marketing and management in college. I learned a great deal about how to lead marketing campaigns and how to manage a small store. I wanted to translate this knowledge in the real world, so I took a job in a small retail chain for two years. I received a broader range of responsibilities than I would have received in a larger chain, and it was a very valuable experience. I am now ready to move into a national chain, where I hope to draw on both my academic and professional experiences."

Analysis of Answer: This answer projects a solid long-term goal that is compatible with the available job. It also takes the opportunity to describe the educational and professional experience the job candidate has garnered in order to prepare for the new position.

What to Avoid: Avoid seeming as if your long-term goals are unrelated to or incompatible with the job you are seeking.

12. Where do you see yourself in five years?

What They Are Looking For: In this question, the interviewer is seeking to assess whether your goals match the opportunities presented by the job opening, and whether your ambitions are attractive to the organization. To answer this question well, consider emphasizing your goal-oriented perspective and your desire to continue to stretch your skills and make valued contributions to the company you seek to join.

Sample Answer: "In five years I hope to be serving as a manager of one of the restaurants in this chain. I would enjoy the challenge of building a strong branch and adapting marketing practices to the local environment, so that my branch would become a high-revenue-earning one. My education has helped me prepare for that by introducing me to broad principles of economics. And the fact that I have worked for a competitor chain gives me a good alternative perspective that I can draw on when working for your company. Because I have already served as a junior assistant manager and have experience building a successful staff and contributing to key marketing campaigns, I will bring good experience to the position of assistant manager that you are offering."

Analysis of Answer: The candidate conveys a medium-term goal that is compatible with the company's interests. The candidate also describes how his or her education and work experience are relevant to the job.

What to Avoid: Avoid presenting a medium-term goal that is incompatible with the needs or interests of the firm you are interviewing with.

13. Where do you see yourself in ten years?

What They Are Looking For: The interviewer wants to know that your longer-term goals are compatible with his or her company's goals or interests. How you answer this question should depend on the type of company or organization you are interviewing with. Clearly, if the company is known for training employees for three years and then sending them out to be independent operators, you might not appear to be a good fit if you imply you wish to be with the company for ten years. However, if the company values long-term employees, you are probably best off implying you intend to stay with the company for a while.

Sample Answer: "In ten years, I hope to be serving as a top CPA of a company like yours. This is why I am highly interested in working for your company. Over the past few years, I have been preparing for this goal. I majored in accounting as an undergraduate and I have begun to prepare to acquire my CPA credential. I had a wonderful opportunity to intern for a small business, as well as for a larger CPA firm. That diversity of experience provides resources for me to draw on in my future work. Now I feel ready to take a longer-term career step by joining a firm that I hope to grow with for years."

Analysis of Answer: This answer is good for a company that is known for hiring job candidates for the long haul. The candidate demonstrates a long-term goal that is compatible with this company's interests and also conveys to the interviewer the educational and professional experience that will help the candidate excel in the company.

What to Avoid: Avoid presenting a career goal that is incompatible with the needs or interests of the firm you are interviewing with.

14. Will you be seeking higher education?

What They Are Looking For: The interviewer wants to hear an answer that is consistent with his or her company's needs or interests. Some companies expect their employees to continue to develop their skills through additional education, while others may want you to advance largely through learning on the job. If you believe the company might be concerned that you will depart quickly in order to earn an advanced degree, you might choose to let the interviewer know you will consider the needs of the firm as you determine later whether or not to pursue further education.

Sample Answer: "I foresee myself gaining many key skills on the job with your company. Whether or not I pursue further education will depend in part upon the needs of your company at the time that I would likely consider further education."

Analysis of Answer: This answer is very cautious. It is more suited to a situation in which the candidate is unclear about whether the company supports higher education among its employees. If the candidate were certain that a company expected its employees to attain higher education, the candidate ideally would have sounded more certain about the desire to seek higher education.

QUESTIONS ABOUT THE AVAILABLE JOB

15. What are you looking for in this job?

What They Are Looking For: In this question, the interviewer is seeking to see if your goals match the opportunities presented in the job for which he or she is interviewing you. Tailor your answer in a way that answers yes to that query. Answer specifically with references to the challenges you hope to meet and the opportunities you want to use to make valued contributions. You can also use this question as a chance to underscore the skills you already have and ways in which this new position might enable you to refine those skills and develop new ones.

Sample Answer: "Given my success as a manager in my telecommunication company start-up, I have developed a good range of project management skills, such as laying out goals and a plan for my team, interacting with clients to meet client needs, and managing work in a way that has enabled my teams to deliver wonderful work products. I enjoyed working at a start-up, but I am now seeking the challenge of using my skills within a larger, more established telecommunications company. The specifics of the job you have advertised are ideal for what I am seeking. I am seeking the challenge of managing larger teams, working with Fortune 500 clients rather than small-business clients, and managing teams in a variety of countries. I thrive in fast-paced environments, so the fact that the job you are offering is expected to involve brisk work is attractive also."

Analysis of Answer: The candidate clearly conveys awareness of the job specifications and demonstrates a match between the candidate's goals and the specifics of the job for which he is interviewing.

What to Avoid: Be sure not to sound as if you are not versed in the specifics of the job that is available. Be certain to do your homework and review as many sources as possible to learn about the job, as well as the roles and responsibilities you would hold in your new position.

16. Why are you seeking to change jobs?

What They Are Looking For: In this question, the interviewer is providing you the chance to paint a picture of yourself with references to your winning attributes. But be careful not to speak too negatively about your present or prior job. You do not want to come across as whining. You want to come across as seeking the new job for positive reasons; you don't want to be perceived as simply fleeing from a job you dislike. Therefore, speak in positive terms about the wonderful opportunities the new job offers you and the ways you will be able to leverage your existing skills while also building new ones.

Sample Answer: "I have worked as a manager in my car rental agency for four years now, and it has been a wonderful experience in terms of the skills I have acquired. I progressed from serving as one of the attendants who took customer information and rented cars to being the manager of all of those attendants in my branch. I have found as I have progressed, however, that my company does not have the culture I was seeking. I understand that your company is more team oriented and stresses that your employees continually undergo human resource training to refine their skills. I am seeking a more collaborative environment in which I can use the many skills I have while also building upon them. The opportunity offered through your job is ideal in my view."

Analysis of Answer: The answer is good because it starts off very positive and stresses the skills of the job candidate. The candidate then explains what is lacking in his or her current job and refers to the strengths offered by the new company. The tone is positive, and the answer presents the candidate as one who seeks continual development and refinement of skills. Those characteristics are valued among most employers.

What to Avoid: Try not to sound too negative when speaking about why you wish to change jobs. You want to appear to be moving toward a positive situation, not running away from a negative one.

17. Does your company know you are looking?

What They Are Looking For: In this question, the interviewer is seeking to get a sense of whether you are honest and straightforward. In most situations, candidates applying for jobs cannot reveal their search to their current employer. However, the interviewer might be pleased to hear that you have laid the groundwork for a departure from your current job by occasionally hinting in open conversation with your superiors that at some point you may wish to look beyond that company. It is usually fine, however, to indicate that while you have spoken openly about your general ambitions in your current workplace, you have not specifically let it be known that you might leave your current job soon.

Sample Answer: "I have a very open and cordial relationship with the executives of my company, and over the years—as I have been promoted and as my skills have developed—I have discussed with my superiors my longer-term goals. They are aware that in time I would be looking outside of our firm. I have therefore laid the groundwork for a departure, but the executives of my firm are not aware that I am currently interviewing for jobs. I will bring that up when I have a job offer in hand."

Analysis of Answer: The response seems candid and aboveboard, so it is likely to leave a positive impression.

What to Avoid: Try to avoid sounding as if you are being underhanded or deceitful by interviewing without the knowledge of your superiors. If you come across that way, the interviewer may question why you are trying to leave your job and begin to think it must be for a negative reason. They might also question whether you are trustworthy.

18. Why are you interested in this firm?

What They Are Looking For: The interviewer will be assessing your response to determine whether there is a fit with what the company offers. This is a question that merits a very specific answer. In responding, draw upon what you have learned about the needs of the firm you are interviewing with and the opportunities afforded by the position you are seeking. You should demonstrate a match between the specific things you say you are seeking and the opportunities and responsibilities offered by the firm. It is also a good practice to weave in references to your existing skills, so the interviewer understands you bring valuable attributes and skills to the table.

Sample Answer: "I have worked as a manager in my clothing retail branch for four years now, and it has been a wonderful experience in terms of the skills I have acquired. I progressed from being one of the cashiers to the manager of all the cashiers in my branch. I have found as I have progressed, however, that my company does not have the culture I was seeking. I understand that your company is more team oriented, encourages input from branch teams who are closest to the customer, and has built its success on customized local marketing campaigns. The experience in your branches seems to be much more rewarding for those with an entrepreneurial spirit, such as myself. Your company is ideal for me because it encourages and embraces creativity and provides a collaborative environment in which I can use and build on my skills."

Analysis of Answer: The candidate appears well versed in the reputation of the company and clearly understands the dimensions through which this company distinguishes itself from competitors. The candidate underscores the match between what he or she is seeking and what the company offers.

What to Avoid: Avoid presenting information that establishes a conflict between your goals and the available job. Avoid seeming as though you are not versed in the specific factors that distinguish the organization you are interviewing with from its competitors.

19. Why are you seeking a change now?

What They Are Looking For: The interviewer is assessing whether the reasons behind your desire to change jobs indicate that you are a suitable choice for the advertised job. This is a question that should receive a specific answer. The interviewer is asking you to indicate why you are ready to move into another position. In many cases, this question is best answered with reference to the progression of skills you have been building and your readiness to take your skills and experiences to the next level. You can also refer to the key attributes that you find attractive in the organization you are interviewing with.

Sample Answer: "I have been a computer and information technology specialist for a start-up company for a number of years now, and I feel I have reached a wonderful spot in my career in which I have maximized my technology learning on the job. I have had the opportunity to use my education to design systems that have supported our corporation well and that have allowed us to do our work well. However, I am seeking a greater challenge now. Since I have knowledge of how to design a system to support business objectives, I want to apply that knowledge in a company that enables me to consult with a wide range of companies that need better technology. Your company offers me the opportunity to use my experience in many creative ways."

Analysis of Answer: The candidate does a wonderful job of touting experiences and successes acquired so far and offers a convincing explanation of why it is time to move to a company that offers greater diversity of experience.

What to Avoid: Try to avoid an answer that sounds unconvincing. Avoid an answer that makes your desired move seem arbitrary or motivated solely by negative factors.

20. What would our company give you that another company would not?

What They Are Looking For: This is a very important question; the interviewer is asking you to state in specific terms why the company you are interviewing with is your first choice or your ideal choice. You should answer this question in detail and well, demonstrating that you are highly familiar with the organization, as well as with the competitors of the organization. It is important to convey that you are choosing this company or organization over others for specific reasons that indicate your interests match the offerings and strengths of the interviewing organization.

Sample Answer: "Your company offers me a number of attractive elements in terms of entrepreneurial experience and the specific culture of your company. I have been a computer and information technology specialist for a large Fortune 500 company for a number of years now, and I feel I have reached a wonderful spot in my career in which I have maximized my technology learning on the job. I have had the opportunity to use my education to design systems that have supported our corporation well and allowed us to do our work well. However, I am seeking a greater entrepreneurial challenge now. I want to apply my knowledge in a small company that needs better technology and in which excellent technology will make a key difference. Your company would offer me that opportunity. In addition, your company is known for innovation and for its collaborative environment. Those are attributes I am seeking in my new company."

Analysis of Answer: The candidate does a wonderful job of touting her experiences and the successes she has had so far. She offers a convincing explanation of why it is time to move to a company that offers entrepreneurial experience. The candidate speaks specifically about the attributes associated with this particular small company, which is a plus. She underscores why those attributes make the company ideal for her.

What to Avoid: Be certain to answer with specifics about the company, since that is specifically what the question asks for. Avoid giving too general an answer.

21. What will you contribute to this workplace?

What They Are Looking For: The interviewer wants specific references to what you hope to contribute and will assess whether your response indicates a match in terms of the needs of the job and/or company. This is an open-ended question that enables you to focus directly on the winning attributes and skills you have to draw on in your potential new work environment. Take the opportunity to direct the conversation toward your strengths and the experiences the interviewing organization will find most attractive.

Sample Answer: "I have been working in sales for five years, and I love to bring fresh thinking and direction to projects I run. In my current company, my ability to continually refine techniques allowed us to increase our customer base and revenues about 20 percent over my first two years. I was promoted to assistant manager. My skills there blossomed, and I became an effective manager of junior sales personnel. I bring to your company my desire to continually improve processes and my history of excellent sales outcomes. I will also contribute to your company excellent team leadership and innovative thinking."

Analysis of Answer: This answer blends information about business successes, skills, and attitudes that presents a positive image of the interviewing candidate.

What to Avoid: Avoid an answer that is too general, such as one that omits reference to specifics about successes or positive attributes.

22. How long do you expect to be at this firm?

What They Are Looking For: In this question, the interviewer is seeking to assess whether your goals match the opportunities and expectations of the organization, and whether your ambitions are attractive to the organization. To answer this question, consider emphasizing your goal-oriented perspective and your desire to continue to stretch your skills and make valued contributions to your work environment. Clearly, if the company is known for training employees for three years and then sending them out to be independent operators, you might not appear to be a good fit if you imply you wish to be with the company in ten years. However, if the company values long-term employees, you are probably best off implying you intend to stay with the company for a while. If appropriate, consider emphasizing that one of your highest priorities is performing excellently for the interviewing company and serving it well for as long as the potential employer needs your valued skills.

Sample Answer: "I hope to stay at your company for the foreseeable future. I know your company puts a high premium on long-term employees who are loyal to the company and willing to grow within the company, taking on management positions as they continue to develop their skill sets. In addition to the culture of your company and the specifics of the job I am seeking, these elements are among the things that most attract me to your company."

Analysis of Answer: This answer responds to the facts the interviewing candidate knows about the expectations of the company with regard to the ideal length of time its employees would stay at the firm. Therefore, this answer likely demonstrates a fit.

What to Avoid: Avoid implying you want to stay a short time at a company that expects its employees to stay for the long term. Similarly, avoid implying you want to stay for a long time at a company that wants shorter-term employees only.

23. Where do you see this industry going?

What They Are Looking For: With this question, the interviewer is asking you to demonstrate that you have done some research about the industry, its trends, opportunities, and challenges. You do not necessarily need to demonstrate that you have a "right" answer to this question. It is usually more important to demonstrate you have done your homework and used information to formulate a coherent, well-reasoned opinion about the industry and where it is headed.

Sample Answer: "The exciting thing about this industry is that it has so many possibilities. From the coverage I have read in finance magazines and major finance journals, I expect to see the mortgage industry seeking to make greater inroads with nontraditional homeowners. That population, from what I understand, is largely untapped. I think that will open opportunities for creative new products and marketing, and the future of the industry is likely therefore to be very exciting."

Analysis of Answer: The candidate demonstrates knowledge about the trends of the industry, taken from reliable sources such as finance magazines and journals.

What to Avoid: Avoid sounding as if you have no sense of the broader trends of the industry. If you appear to have some knowledge about industry directions, you will create a better impression.

24. How do you view our company?

What They Are Looking For: The interviewer is asking you to comment on the qualities you like about the company. You might wish to characterize the company both in its own right and relative to competitors in its field.

Sample Answer: "I view your company as the ideal choice for me. From my record in college, you can see that I helped to push forward innovative research in the sciences, and that I enjoyed working on team projects. I am looking for a high technology company that is known for innovation and that spearheads research on leading-edge products for hospitals. In the past five years, your company has led the way in developing products to improve imaging in medical scanning devices. I have read a great deal about how those innovative products have improved health care. I know your company is also currently investing a great deal of research and development money into developing a new generation of products that can improve medical testing techniques. Given your company's emphasis on innovation and my own commitment to contributing to advances in medicine through technology, your company is ideal for me. I have also spoken with several of your employees, and from our conversations I know that your corporate culture, which emphasizes teamwork and collaboration with partner companies, is also ideal for me."

Analysis of Answer: Through this answer, the candidate clearly demonstrates that he is aware of the company's reputation for innovation and is also aware of the range of products that the company has produced recently, the effects of those products in the health care arena, and the future direction of the company in terms of research and development. This is likely to impress the interviewer. In addition, the candidate took the time to speak with employees of the company to get a sense of the corporate culture. This demonstrates initiative as well as the candidate's serious interest in ensuring that this company is the right choice for him. The interviewer will no doubt believe that this candidate is one who is serious and enthusiastic about joining his or her company.

What to Avoid: Avoid issuing such nonspecific comments that you cause the interviewer to question whether you have taken the time to learn a great deal about the company. If the interviewer thinks you have not researched the company well, he or she is prone to believe that you are not serious about joining and perhaps may have another employer as your first choice.

25. What do you consider our mission to be?

What They Are Looking For: The interviewer is asking you to demonstrate that you have done your homework and are familiar with the mission statement and broad activities of the organization. Draw on the research you have done to summarize the mission for the interviewer.

Sample Answer: "I admire your company because its mission is to diversify the financial resources available to lower-income individuals by developing new financial instruments and marketing those instruments to large lending institutions. I am seeking a company that specializes in finance but that has a social mission, and one that engages in new areas of finance. Given this, I was immediately drawn to this company."

Analysis of Answer: The candidate does a wonderful job of demonstrating familiarity with the mission of the company and stresses that the institution offers the attributes he or she has been seeking in a company.

What to Avoid: Know what a company's mission is before interviewing, because this helps to demonstrate you have considered the company carefully. Try not to interview without having that basic information about the company and its goals.

26. Summarize what you consider to be the main aspects of the job we are offering.

What They Are Looking For: The interviewer is asking you to demonstrate that you have done your homework and are familiar with the roles and responsibilities associated with the available job. Draw on the research you have done to summarize the mission for the interviewer.

Sample Answer: "As I understand it, you are offering a position in which an experienced administrative assistant will be able to join a team and help design new programs to increase the efficiency of one of your slower-growing divisions. The position will involve analysis of the reasons for the division's inefficiency, streamlining projects, completing implementation, and training new administrative personnel. I am very drawn to this position. I have six years of experience as an administrative assistant in a very successful large company. I would look forward to applying what I have learned to your organization, and I believe my perspectives can help identify the sources of inefficiency as well as the ways we can streamline activities. Because I am also very good with people and have trained many of our new employees, I believe I am ideally suited for this position."

Analysis of Answer: The answer is good in that it clearly demonstrates that this candidate is familiar with all of the key elements of the job. The candidate takes the opportunity to demonstrate a match between the position offered and the candidate's credentials.

What to Avoid: You must avoid sounding as if you have no understanding of the roles and responsibilities associated with the job for which you are interviewing.

27. What do you perceive as the negatives about this firm?

What They Are Looking For: The interviewer is giving you the chance to assure him or her that you do not see significant negatives about the interviewing company that might make you dislike it or otherwise make you a poor choice for the job. Be careful with this question. All too often, job candidates answer such questions too frankly. Remember, your goal at this stage is to get the job. The well-known negatives about the firm do not necessarily need to be brought up here. In all probability, the interviewer may believe that if you bring up those well-known negatives, your concern may indicate that you are not a good fit for the organization. It is probably best to err on the side of caution.

Sample Answer: "Given what I am looking for in a company, I do not see huge negatives about your firm. I am looking for a small company based in a small urban setting that focuses on new technologies in the area of health care. Some people may feel that a small company is not right for them or that a small urban environment is not ideal. For me, those are key pluses."

Analysis of Answer: The answer is good in that it acknowledges what might cause some candidates to choose to forgo the company offering the job, but it underscores that those very attributes are attractive to the candidate.

What to Avoid: Avoid sounding as though the main negatives of the company are factors that might make you dislike the job for which you are interviewing.

28. What do you perceive as the negatives about this position?

What They Are Looking For: The interviewer is giving you the chance to assure him or her that you do not see significant negatives about the job that will make you dislike it or otherwise make you a poor choice. Be careful with this question. All too often, job candidates answer such queries too openly. Your goal at this stage is to land the job offer. The interviewer may believe that if you bring up well-known negatives about the job, your concern may indicate that you are not a good fit for the position. It is probably best to be cautious in your response.

Sample Answer: "Given what I am looking for in a company, I do not see huge negatives in the position. I am looking for a challenging environment in which I can help manage a team to meet the needs of our clients. I am also looking for a company that is expanding into a new marketplace. This company and this position provide those attributes. Some people may view the brisk pace of your advertised managerial position to be a burden, but I enjoy challenges and am good at dealing with stressful situations and overcoming obstacles in order to achieve success."

Analysis of Answer: The answer is good in that it emphasizes areas where the company and the advertised job are a good match with the candidate. The candidate also acknowledges what many people might consider to be a negative of the specific position advertised, while underscoring that this is not a negative for the candidate.

What to Avoid: Avoid sounding as though the main negative of the available job is a major factor that might cause you to dislike the position for which you are interviewing.

QUESTIONS ABOUT YOUR EDUCATION

29. Why did you choose the college you attended?

What They Are Looking For: The interviewer is probably genuinely interested in your answer but will also be assessing which characteristics you highlight and whether they indicate a fit with the company or advertised job. This open-ended question gives you a chance to refer to your key attractive attributes, college experiences, and skills. You therefore can paint an excellent picture of your personality and character, as well as of your skills, knowledge, and experiences.

Sample Answer: "Four key factors attracted me to my college: its reputation for excellence, its location, its student body, and its curriculum. I enjoy dynamic environments with a lot of diversity, where people are serious about exploring ideas in depth. I also like being near a big city, where I can enjoy the history and cultural attractions. My college gave me all of these things. There I met people from all over the world, and I studied with professors who were the best in their field. I also enjoyed living near New York, where I could visit famous museums and attend plays. This environment motivated me and accounts for why I excelled not only academically but also through leadership as the president of the Women's Group."

Analysis of Answer: The answer does a great job of weaving in information about the interviewing candidate's winning personality characteristics and values. The candidate also refers to a leadership position, which is a plus.

What to Avoid: Try to avoid an answer that does not take the opportunity to weave in information about your winning attributes and achievements in college.

30. How did you like your undergraduate institution?

What They Are Looking For: The interviewer will be assessing which characteristics you liked or disliked, to determine whether your personality and preferences make you a good choice for the available job and interviewing company. This question gives you a chance to refer to your key attractive attributes, college experiences, and skills. You therefore can paint an excellent picture of your personality and character, as well as of your skills, knowledge, and experiences. You should emphasize the positive aspects of your experience and minimize references to the negatives, unless there is a good reason for elaborating on them. You want to present your education as an asset, so speaking about it in positive terms that underscore the valuable knowledge and skills you picked up, the opportunities to explore new ideas, and the students you interacted with (among other things) helps you ensure the interviewer sees your education as a plus.

Sample Answer: "I enjoy dynamic environments with a diversity of ideas and people and in which there are many ways to deepen my knowledge and to make good contributions. My college gave me all of these things, so it was a wonderful choice. My college attracts talented students from all over the United States and the world, and as a liberal arts college, it offers a wide array of majors. I enjoyed deepening my knowledge in education not only through great courses but also through fieldwork. I also liked making contributions by serving as the vice president of the Education for Rosemont group, which sent students into a rural area to offer support to teachers in that area."

Analysis of Answer: The answer does a great job of weaving in information about the interviewing candidate's winning personality characteristics and values. The candidate also refers to a leadership position, which is a plus.

What to Avoid: Try to avoid an answer that is flat and misses the opportunity to weave in information about your winning attributes and achievements in college.

31. What is the most distinct contribution you made to your undergraduate institution?

What They Are Looking For: The interviewer is seeking to find out how significant your presence was within your college. This will give him or her a sense of how you will contribute at the interviewer's organization. The interviewer is also offering you a chance to use a concrete accomplishment to speak about your key attractive attributes, skills, and knowledge and how you were able to draw on these to make a difference in an organization. Use this as an opportunity to underscore important themes about your abilities, positive attitude, and potential for success.

Sample Answer: "My most distinct contribution was starting a tutoring group called College Support. Being from a rural environment, I had a difficult time adjusting to my urban college at first. I wished I had had more support in my freshman year. Watching others struggle the same way motivated me to start College Support. I like to take the initiative to make positive changes when I see significant problems. College Support matched upper-class students, who were willing to tutor for free, with freshmen who were having difficulties. I helped the organization grow to 100 tutors and over 150 freshmen participants. I learned a great deal about leadership through my work, as well as about marketing and management. I also enjoyed the many thank-yous from freshmen who were grateful to have a support network to draw on when they arrived on campus."

Analysis of Answer: The answer does a wonderful job of referring to the candidate's achievement in business-relevant terms. It also portrays the candidate as having initiative and motivation. The candidate has likely created a highly favorable impression with the interviewer.

What to Avoid: Avoid saying that you made no distinct contribution to your school! Even if you were not involved in campus activities, your contributions to class discussions might be noteworthy.

32. Explain this series of poor grades you received in school.

What They Are Looking For: The interviewer is seeking to have you explain poor grades and assure him or her that the grades are not a reflection of a current lack of motivation, dedication, or ability to perform.

Sample Answer: "Unfortunately, when I was in college I was not focused on my future. I saw college as a time to explore friendships, campus activities, and cultural events, but not as a time to focus on my studies. I don't make excuses for the poor grades. What I have tried to do since I have become more focused and dedicated to my future is to build a new record of achievement. You see that I have taken numerous courses in the extension school of a local college to deepen my knowledge, as well as to demonstrate my true capabilities. You can also see that I have received numerous professional certifications that attest to my abilities. The best indicator of my current abilities is my strong record in my current job, as indicated by my recent promotion. I hope that these other factors will demonstrate that you can count on me to perform excellently at your organization."

Analysis of Answer: The tone of the response is not defensive, and it acknowledges and explains the poor grades without trying to make an excuse for them. The candidate then shifts the conversation to focus on the more recent record of achievements, to assure the interviewer of the candidate's current focus, dedication, and abilities.

What to Avoid: Do not sound defensive. Refer to your efforts to establish a new record that can minimize or negate the importance of your poor grades.

33. Why did you choose this major?

What They Are Looking For: The interviewer wants you to stress qualities that are relevant to the job for which you are interviewing. Candidates who have backgrounds that are not directly relevant to the position they are applying for often get defensive about this question. However, as demonstrated in early parts of this book, it is possible to gain relevant skills through a wide range of majors. Therefore, if you are applying for a business position without a business or economics education, you should still speak of your major in positive terms, underscoring the broader skills that transcend a particular major and can allow you to excel in the advertised position. Use this as an opportunity to underscore important themes about your abilities, your skills, and the many experiences you can draw on to excel within the interviewing organization.

Sample Answer: "I was looking for a major that enabled me to test new ideas and explore complex problems, while also helping to prepare me for a future career. Engineering was a wonderful choice, because not only did I work on projects in leading areas of engineering and design, but the rigors of the major also made me very disciplined and a sharp problem solver. I feel very prepared now to embark on my business career because I can use my problem-solving and analytical skills."

Analysis of Answer: The candidate makes his engineering major relevant to business in terms of projects and design and in terms of broader skills such as problem solving. That is a good blend.

What to Avoid: If possible, avoid portraying your major as not relevant in any way to the advertised job.

34. In what ways do you believe your undergraduate major helped prepare you for this position?

What They Are Looking For: The interviewer would like to hear specifics about how your education has helped to make you qualified for the available job. Like Question 33, this question gives you an opportunity to demonstrate that you attained relevant skills for your job through your undergraduate education. Therefore, even if you are applying for a business position without a business or economics education, you can still use this question as a chance to talk about your major in positive terms, emphasizing the broad skills that transcend a particular major and will enable you to distinguish yourself with excellent performance in the advertised job. Use this question as an opportunity to underscore skills, knowledge, and experiences that will help you to be an excellent employee.

Sample Answer: "As a math major, I had to complete many upper-level applied mathematical courses that required extensive research and teamwork. All of those elements—mathematics, research, and teamwork—make me very prepared for my new finance career. In the area of finance, math skills, the ability to work with data, and analytical skills are key. Likewise, your finance company completes much of its work in teams and through research. The research and team skills I already have will enable me to excel here."

Analysis of Answer: The candidate makes the college major relevant not only in terms of content but also in terms of broader skills. That is a good blend.

What to Avoid: If possible, avoid portraying your major as not relevant in any way to the available job.

35. What was your favorite course in college?

What They Are Looking For: The interviewer will assess the personality qualities you reveal through your response. Use this opportunity to highlight the positive attributes the interviewing organization will value, such as curiosity and a desire to be challenged. The course content might also be relevant. As you talk about your favorite course, use business-relevant terms to explain why you enjoyed it.

Sample Answer: "My favorite class was one about public policy in the area of farm subsidies. It sounds a bit boring perhaps, but what I enjoyed was that this class required that I draw on many of the skills I had developed as a freshman and a sophomore—research skills, economics knowledge, math skills, modeling, and analytical reasoning—to work with a team of students to produce a recommendation about how to alter current farm subsidy levels. After we completed a small report about this, we had the opportunity to present our findings to public policy makers. The blend of drawing on such a broad mix of skills and presenting a compelling set of findings was very exciting. I know I will be able to complete similar work in your company's setting, which is why I would look forward to the opportunity."

Analysis of Answer: The candidate comes across as someone who enjoys bringing a wide range of tools to bear on issues, and who is pleasant to work with in teams. The positive, upbeat nature of the response leaves a favorable impression. Likewise, the candidate clearly conveys the broad range of skills he developed in college.

What to Avoid: Avoid making a reference to a course that will be seen as having very little relevance or that does not reveal desirable traits about your personality.

QUESTIONS ABOUT YOUR QUALIFICATIONS

36. What attributes will make you a valued presence at our company?

What They Are Looking For: The interviewer wants to see whether you can articulate your strengths clearly and whether these attributes will make you ideal for the advertised position. This is an open-ended question that gives you latitude to focus on your core attributes, your skills, and some of your accomplishments in prior positions that you will be able to draw on in the new position. Try to direct the conversation toward the strengths and skills that the interviewer will find most attractive, given the responsibilities of the position for which you are interviewing.

Sample Answer: "I offer a great deal both in terms of my personal attributes and in terms of my professional work record. In terms of my personal attributes, I am goal oriented and committed to achieving strong results. That has helped me to excel in my job. For instance, in the first two years of my work as the manager of a dental clinic, I have helped to expand our customer base by 40 percent. I also designed marketing schemes that proved very effective. I bring to your company my record of achievements and the attributes that made them possible."

Analysis of Answer: The answer provides a good blend of information about skills and accomplishments.

What to Avoid: Do not fail to articulate your winning attributes. Make sure they demonstrate a fit with the company.

37. In what areas do you need to develop professionally?

What They Are Looking For: The interviewer is seeking a candid answer that indicates how you hope to grow but one that does not undermine the notion that you are suitable for the available job. All employees have ways in which they can develop their skills and deepen their experiences. Your answer to this question should acknowledge that and name an area in which you would like to refine your skills. If there is a clear weakness about your professional record, you might carefully acknowledge that also, but do so after quickly referring to the many skills you bring to the table.

Sample Answer: "The way I need to develop professionally is to gain more experience managing large teams. In the past, I excelled in my work as an associate and then as a project leader. In my position as project leader, I was in charge of teams of four to six associates. I would define the scope of our work, check the work of the associates, and provide feedback on the work. I mastered the art of being a good team leader, but I would like to expand my experience to include larger teams and multiple teams."

Analysis of Answer: This answer pinpoints something that is relatively harmless. By stating that he or she has mastered the art of team leadership, the candidate presents this professional development area merely needing to be further expanded. It is a minor weakness, therefore an area in which the candidate does not yet have experience. This answer is not likely to undercut the candidate in the interview process unless the job description requires experience with managing large teams.

What to Avoid: Try to avoid focusing on an area that is central to the skills you need in order to excel in the job for which you are applying.

38. What is your greatest professional weakness?

What They Are Looking For: The interviewer is looking for a candid description that indicates an area of weakness. He or she wants to make sure your weakness is not central to the skills you will need to succeed in the advertised position. Pinpoint an area you wish to improve (and one that hopefully you are currently working on). All employees have ways in which they can strengthen their performance. However, there is usually no need to speak at length about a weakness, and it is often best to choose something that is somewhat harmless and not central to the skills you must use to excel in the position for which you are interviewing.

Sample Answer: "My greatest professional weakness is working too hard. I am passionate about what I do, but I have to keep balance in my life and also allow my team members to maintain balance in their lives. So prioritizing work and setting clear limits to the scope of our work is always key. I have to make sure to do that so as to keep from working my teams too hard."

Analysis of Answer: This is a bit of a generic answer—one that interviewers no doubt hear often. However, it is also a harmless answer. Few employers will fault you for working too hard. For that reason, it is usually a safe answer.

What to Avoid: Avoid mentioning a weakness that is central to the skills you need in order to excel in the job for which you are applying or that presents you as a professional who is hard to work with.

39. What is your greatest professional strength?

What They Are Looking For: The interviewer is looking for you to elaborate on a broad strength that is well supported by your résumé and highly relevant to the job you are applying for. If you highlight that sort of strength, you can help create the notion that you are a good match for the available job.

Sample Answer: "My greatest professional strength is innovation. I love bringing fresh, novel ideas to issues and to drawing on the talents of dynamic colleagues in order to bring creativity to our work. My innovation enabled me to design new management processes for my company and to blend those with technological tools. Given that the job that I am interviewing for requires innovation, I believe I am a good choice for the position."

Analysis of Answer: This answer does a good job of focusing on an attribute that is critical for success in the advertised job. The candidate also offers an example of his or her innovation and its results, which makes the importance of the attribute more concrete.

What to Avoid: Avoid focusing on an attribute that lacks relevance to the job you are trying to secure.

40. What could you have improved about your performance in your last job?

What They Are Looking For: The interviewer is looking for a description of an area in which you need to improve but he or she is seeking to ensure that it is not central to the position for which you are applying. Choose an area of performance that is not central to the skills you must use excellently to distinguish yourself in the job for which you are applying. You don't want to undercut the notion that you are a good match for the available job.

Sample Answer: "My performance could have been improved if I had worked my team a little less hard. I tend to be passionate about what I do, but I have to keep balance in my life. I also must remember to allow my team members to maintain balance in their lives. So prioritizing work and setting clear limits to our work is always key. I kept our work level brisk in my last project, and we succeeded, helping our client to save thousands of dollars with a new strategic solution. But I believe we could have done equally as well while paring down our work hours a bit."

Analysis of Answer: This is a cautious answer. Few employers will fault you for working too hard. Because the candidate affirms that the team was successful, the fact that the team worked too hard will likely be seen in a less negative light.

What to Avoid: Avoid naming a performance area that is central to the skills you must use to excel in the new job.

41. If there is something we might be concerned about in your résumé, what would it be?

What They Are Looking For: Often when an interviewer asks this question, there is a specific issue of concern. The interviewer wants you to acknowledge that issue and then explain why that issue will not be an obstacle to your ability to perform excellently in the job for which you are interviewing.

Sample Answer: "My résumé indicates that it took me seven years to graduate from college. That may be a point of concern for you. Unfortunately, I was working nearly thirty hours per week during college, and during my last two years, I had to work full-time in order to earn my tuition. With the stress of working and the difficulty of my major, I decided to take a smaller course load so that I would not undercut my ability to do well. You can see my GPA remained strong, so I believe I made a good decision. The promotions I received during my work at that time also show that I was quite motivated in my professional work in spite of the hardship of working during my college years."

Analysis of Answer: The candidate does not respond defensively, which is good. Also, the candidate acknowledges the perceived weakness and is prepared to explain it. The candidate assures the interviewer that many other indicators, including his strong GPA, attest to his strong commitment and abilities.

What to Avoid: Try not to sound defensive when you respond, and offer a convincing explanation of the weakness. Also, try to point the interviewer to your successes so that the interviewer might conclude that the weakness on your résumé should not determine the interview's outcome.

42. We have found that people with your training have difficulty at our company. Is there any reason why you think you will fare better?

What They Are Looking For: The interviewer is giving you the opportunity to highlight the range of skills and experiences that can help you succeed in your new position.

Sample Answer: "I can only convey to you what to expect of my own performance. As I hope my record indicates, I have worked very hard to build an excellent record in every aspect possible, from academics to professional work experience. My high GPA indicates to you how seriously I take my work and how interested I am in learning. It also indicates I have strong analytical skills. My professional experience, in which I have received two promotions over three years, also demonstrates that my superiors have seen me as a top performer among my peers and have entrusted me with expanding responsibilities. With the skills I have developed in the areas of financial analysis and management, I bring a solid record to build upon at your company, and I believe my dedication will enable me to excel."

Analysis of Answer: The answer is not defensive and does a good job of highlighting the candidate's strengths and dedication.

What to Avoid: Don't get defensive about the phrasing of this question. Take the chance to steer the conversation directly to your winning attributes, skills, and experiences.

43. You seem overqualified for this position. We think you may have a problem with the reduction in your responsibilities. What do you think about this?

What They Are Looking For: Appearing overqualified can pose a considerable problem in the interviewing process, as the hiring company may feel you will not remain in the position long or might be reluctant to operate within the limits of your designated roles. One of the best ways to address this is to draw attention to the many attractive aspects of the position that have prompted you to apply for the position, and to convey convincingly that you are certain the position is ideal for you.

Sample Answer: "In my company, I have progressed to the position of manager, where I have been in charge of seven team members and very complex projects. However, with your company I will move into a somewhat different product area with a different customer base. I have much to learn about the new marketing techniques that should be used in this new area. I see room for my own growth in the position you offer. On top of this, because your company offers the culture and environment I have been seeking, I am excited about the prospects of this new position. I see the position of assistant manager as one that I will greatly enjoy."

Analysis of Answer: This answer does a good job of explaining how the candidate sees room to grow and also points to other attractive factors about the company that make the position attractive.

What to Avoid: Don't get defensive about the phrasing of this question. Take the chance to steer the conversation directly to your winning attributes, skills, and experiences, as well as the reasons why the available job is precisely what you are looking for.

QUESTIONS ABOUT YOUR LEADERSHIP

44. Tell me about a situation at work in which you led a team well.

What They Are Looking For: In this question, the interviewer is trying to learn whether you are familiar with broad, effective leadership practices. You should refer to well-established leadership best practices, such as setting goals, delegating work well, and managing the work of your team members effectively.

Sample Answer: "In my current position as a team manager, I recently led a successful transaction with a client in which we helped design a computing system that enabled the client to catalog and track inventory across 100 branch locations. The project was very complex. Three things enabled me to lead my team wonderfully. First, I outlined carefully and clearly the scope of the project. Second, I set goals for us to attain at various points in the project and kept our work on track. And third, I created a positive environment in which the team members were willing to go the extra distance. We delivered the project on time and without flaws."

Analysis of Answer: This is a structured answer with concrete specifics about what enables the candidate to lead teams well.

What to Avoid: Avoid a situation in which you do not have an example to present. Normally, if asked, this question is relatively important, so you should have thought through ahead of time a good leadership example upon which you can elaborate.

45. Tell me about a situation at work in which you experienced conflict and how you resolved it.

What They Are Looking For: In this question, the interviewer is trying to learn whether you are familiar with broad, effective conflict-management practices. You might want to refer to well-established best practices for conflict management, such as listening objectively to the parties involved, creating an open dialogue to resolve the problem, and helping to facilitate compromise.

Sample Answer: "In my current position as a sales manager, our division began to experience falling revenue, and executives did not know who was responsible for the downturn. Infighting began in our division, and it was bad for morale. I suggested that all of the sales managers get together and decide how to assign roles with more clear responsibilities. We redefined our roles and also began to hold more frequent meetings to help us work together in designing effective sales strategies. By bringing people to the table to talk through the problem, assign clearer roles, and to design programs to improve the situation, I helped quell tensions. We were able to slow some of the decline in our sales and win additional business."

Analysis of Answer: This is a structured answer with concrete specifics about techniques the candidate used to smooth over a tense situation. The candidate conveys her ability to manage conflict.

What to Avoid: Be ready to elaborate on conflict-management practices or principles. Avoid a situation in which you cannot articulate best practices that have worked for you.

46. Describe a situation in which you faced an ethical challenge in the workplace and how you resolved it.

What They Are Looking For: In the post-Enron environment, some interviewers will be interested to hear about your ethics and the degree to which you can be counted on to make sound ethical decisions. Many job candidates have a hard time coming up with a response to this question, so take time to consider an example if you think this question may come up in your interview. Choose an example that enables you to demonstrate you have strong ethics or that when you had a chance, you chose not to participate in poor behavior.

Sample Answer: "I was in a situation in which I believed a woman in our company was being discriminated against in the promotion process. I work in a heavily male-dominated company, and some of the executives have deep biases. I had to decide whether to keep quiet about this or engage the executives about the rumors that were beginning to spread about overt gender discrimination. I chose to address the issue, and with the open dialogue I initiated, steps were put in place to ensure a more bias-free evaluation and promotion process."

Analysis of Answer: This is a good example, as it shows the candidate in a positive light in an area—gender discrimination—in which many people will agree that assertive action is commendable.

What to Avoid: Avoid conveying information that indicates you engaged in unethical behavior. You should seek to highlight a situation in which you acted in an upstanding manner.

47. How do you behave in teams?

What They Are Looking For: Asking how you behave in teams may be a way for the interviewer to determine whether others in the organization will be able to work well with you. You should convey to the interviewer that you understand broad principles of good team participation, such as understanding your designated role on a team or of delivering excellent work on time.

Sample Answer: "How I behave in teams is a function of my role on the team. When I am appointed the team leader, I set direction and give good feedback as our work progresses. When I am a team participant and not its leader, I respect the role of the team leader, and I deliver high-quality work on schedule. I also help the team leader with the tasks that can bring us success, such as setting direction and creating a positive atmosphere on the team."

Analysis of Answer: The answer is good because the candidate offers concrete information about what he does to be a good team leader and participant. This response also indicates the candidate can function well as either a leader or a team member.

What to Avoid: Be able to make reference to some useful best practices of team participation that have worked for you. Try to avoid creating the impression that you overstep your bounds if you are a team member; indicate that you respect the team leader's role. Try not to create the impression that you are too controlling or authoritarian if you are the team leader.

48. What is your management style?

What They Are Looking For: Asking how you manage people can be a way for the interviewer to determine whether you are someone with whom others enjoy working. While this question has no "right" answer, you should convey to the interviewer that you understand the value of listening to the opinions and views of others and of creating an environment in which coworkers are encouraged to participate.

Sample Answer: "As a manager, I am straightforward and to the point. I give clear directions and honest feedback. I encourage cooperation among my staff, and I help to develop the skills of my subordinates, since I consider professional development to be a core part of my job."

Analysis of Answer: This is a good description of a management style and portrays this candidate as a hands-on, effective, and pleasant manager.

What to Avoid: Avoid coming across as dictatorial—as someone who issues orders and does not attempt to receive input from others in your management process. Also avoid a situation in which you are unable to articulate a coherent management style.

49. Tell me about a time when you exhibited initiative.

What They Are Looking For: Some interviewers would like to understand whether you can be counted on to push forward-thinking or novel ideas in the workplace, or to help manage difficult situations when they arise. If you think this question will arise, think of an example in which you helped develop and implement a change or project that improved the work or atmosphere of your organization.

Sample Answer: "In our company, many sales staff members believed that a number of innovative ideas generated by the salespeople—who are our point of contact with the customers—never made it up to management. I developed a feedback system and a series of periodic lunches between key sales staff and executives, which opened the doors for the two sets of professionals to meet regularly and exchange ideas and information. As a result, more innovative ideas were offered to our executives, who could develop and implement them. This also enabled executives to stay abreast of the needs and feedback of our customers."

Analysis of Answer: This is a good answer that shows how this candidate took the initiative to implement an improvement in the workplace. It also demonstrates the candidate's ability to work with both sales staff and executives. The response paints a very positive picture of the candidate.

What to Avoid: Avoid coming across as someone who must be prodded to take leadership actions or to develop innovative ideas. Conversely, try to ensure that you don't come across as someone who overreaches his or her roles and interferes with the work of others.

50. How do you deal with stressful situations at work?

What They Are Looking For: In this question, the interviewer is trying to assess whether you know broad principles about stress management. If so, this implies you can use that knowledge to the benefit of both yourself and others at work. You should refer to constructive ways in which you deal with stress.

Sample Answer: "To deal with stressful situations, I always take time at the end of a day to reflect upon the day's events and to analyze what I could have done better. When I notice prolonged problems, I take action to bring about change. I have found that taking time to reflect is a key part of managing stress."

Analysis of Answer: This example portrays the candidate as thoughtful and levelheaded. He also comes across as very action-oriented.

What to Avoid: Avoid seeming as if you do not know how to handle stress.

51. How do you define success in a team project?

What They Are Looking For: In this question, the interviewer is trying to assess whether you value professional work in ways that are meaningful for the organization. The emphasis the interviewer will want to hear in your response may depend upon the nature of the company or organization. The answer you might give to the interviewer for a nonprofit job, for instance, may vary from the answer you might give to the interviewer representing a for-profit corporation.

Sample Answer: "I measure success in terms of producing excellent work for my company's clients and in terms of the professional development I am able to provide for my team members. Excellent work for our clients is important to keeping my company positioned well in its field. Helping my team members develop professionally is one of the most important goals in my role as a manager. When I was more junior, others made certain that I stretched my skills and excelled, so I enjoy doing the same for others."

Analysis of Answer: This answer is very positive and demonstrates that the candidate values two things most organizations also value: customers and employees.

What to Avoid: Avoid appearing greedy or self-centered, by answering something like "I measure success by the size of my bonus at the end of the year." In most situations, such an answer will be viewed unfavorably.

52. Describe an unsuccessful project you have been involved with at work, and assess why it was not successful.

What They Are Looking For: This question can be tricky. The interviewer is asking you to demonstrate that you know how to learn from mistakes, but you do not want to offer an extreme mistake that you made that might have cost your company money, clients, or any other valued resource. Choose something relatively harmless in which you can demonstrate your ability to learn from a mistake without undercutting the image of your own strong leadership or professional abilities.

Sample Answer: "When I was first hired by my firm, I was assigned to a project with a manager who was a poor communicator and had a quick temper. On the team, members were afraid to approach him when they experienced problems, and morale was low. Our work was rather bland. From this unsuccessful experience, I learned a great deal about what not to do as I progressed in my career. Since I have become a manager, I have always made sure to establish strong relationships with my team members and to ensure they are comfortable approaching me. These practices have helped to make my teams excellent at producing high-quality work."

Analysis of Answer: This answer is good because the candidate does not choose an example that puts the candidate at fault for the unsuccessful project. It is also good because the candidate stresses the lessons learned from the situation and elaborates on how she has applied those lessons since becoming a manager.

What to Avoid: Avoid speaking about a situation in which you were at fault for a mistake that was highly costly to your company.

53. How do you help ensure that your employees meet project deadlines?

What They Are Looking For: The interviewer is asking you to explain what sorts of techniques you use to inspire employees to perform well. You should focus mostly on positive incentives or techniques, such as coaching team members or reviewing work periodically to ensure short-term goals are being met.

Sample Answer: "To make sure my employees meet designated deadlines, I meet with them periodically and manage them according to their needs. Some of them require that I check their work products often. Others work better with greater latitude. By checking work and making sure we are meeting short-term deadlines, I ensure that we stay on schedule."

Analysis of Answer: The clarity of the answer demonstrates that this candidate knows a great deal about managing staff. The fact that the candidate highlights specific practices to answer the question will likely impress the interviewer.

What to Avoid: Avoid answering in a manner that is too general. Specifics are usually better suited to answering this question.

54. How do you motivate subordinates?

What They Are Looking For: The interviewer is asking you to explain what sorts of techniques you use to motivate employees. You should focus mostly on positive incentives or techniques, such as coaching team members.

Sample Answer: "My subordinates are motivated by different things. I have come to know each of them well, so I understand what motivates each of them. Some employees are motivated by increasing amounts of responsibility. Others are motivated by financial rewards. So I have learned to carve the incentives in ways that each staff member appreciates."

Analysis of Answer: This answer is thoughtful and demonstrates that the candidate has developed leadership techniques that have worked. The candidate will likely impress the interviewer, given the attention to developing good relationships with subordinates and managing employees individually.

What to Avoid: Avoid sounding as if you do not know how to motivate subordinates. Avoid sounding as if you employ only negative incentives to motivate subordinates.

55. Tell me about a time when you solved an important problem in the workplace.

What They Are Looking For: The interviewer is looking for you to demonstrate that you know how to approach problem solving, an important part of work and teamwork today. Using phrases such as "I analyzed the key factors" or "I secured input from the relevant parties" can help give a response the texture the interviewer may be hoping for.

Sample Answer: "I work for an international company, and since marketing is centralized in the head office, it is important that we understand the needs of our local offices. For some reason, technology within our company had not been deployed well to ease the process of communicating among all of our international branches. I found my work very difficult and ineffective as a result. I did some research and presented my findings to management, recommending that we purchase and implement a technology system to support the company's marketing operations. My presentation impressed management, and we implemented the system. Our marketing efforts are now much more timely and effective, resulting in higher sales in many of the branches."

Analysis of Answer: The candidate replies with a specific example that demonstrates initiative in a key area of the company. This example also demonstrates excellent research abilities and an ability to make a persuasive presentation, thereby underscoring the candidate's skills. This answer is likely to produce a very positive response from the interviewer.

What to Avoid: Avoid sounding as if you are unfamiliar with key practices associated with problem solving.

56. What is the central skill you employ in your current job?

What They Are Looking For: The interviewer is probing to assess whether there is a fit between the skill you currently employ and the skills needed for success in the advertised job. When answering this question, consider what skill will be central to the job you are interviewing for. When speaking about the skill you use in your current job, speak in terms that are directly relevant to the job you are seeking.

Sample Answer: "Effective time management is the skill I use the most in my current job. The pace of our work is brisk and demanding, and I oversee the work of twenty employees. At least four teams are operating in my group at any given time. My role is to coordinate and oversee the work and to ensure that all work comes together so we can attain our quarterly goals. To do that, I make sure to meet with all team members and refine timelines, and to organize activities well. I understand that in the position for which I am interviewing, the pace is equally demanding. I believe I will be able to meet the challenge of that brisk pace very well."

Analysis of Answer: This provides a concrete answer and does a good job of relating the current skill employed by the candidate to the skill needed to excel in the new job.

What to Avoid: Avoid speaking about a skill that is not relevant to the position you are interviewing for. You are aiming to make your experience look relevant.

57. How do you balance client needs with company goals?

What They Are Looking For: The interviewer wants to assess whether you know how to balance the needs of the clients with the goals of your company—considerations that do not always pull in the same direction.

Sample Answer: "I have been fortunate because in most cases there has been no conflict between our clients' needs and our company's goals. Recognizing that I have a responsibility both to my clients and my company, I would need to consider carefully any request in which a client was asking me to do something that undercut my company's goals. I would have to consider how deep the conflict was and how important this client was to the company. At the end of the day, if forced to choose, I would confer with my supervisors and likely choose my company's best interests while continuing to act in a highly ethical manner toward the client."

Analysis of Answer: This response is candid and shows that the candidate knows how to weigh the company's interests against the interests of the client. The fact that the candidate affirms a commitment to act in a highly ethical manner is a plus.

What to Avoid: Avoid sounding as if you would make a hasty decision rather than a thoughtful one.

58. How do you deal with difficult clients?

What They Are Looking For: The interviewer wants to know that you know how to deal with tense situations in which you must try to address client concerns and please your difficult clients. The interviewer may also want to hear you acknowledge that you know how to set limits on pleasing difficult clients when the actions required to please such clients are not in the best interests of your company.

Sample Answer: "I have found over time that the best way to deal with difficult clients is to meet with key client representatives individually, convey a sincere intention to work with them to attain excellent outcomes, and keep the dialogue with them open and frank. I make sure they understand they can communicate with me openly and that I am receptive to trying to address their concerns. I follow up with periodic phone calls to keep things progressing smoothly."

Analysis of Answer: The candidate sounds well versed in how to handle difficult clients and is able to pinpoint specific techniques that have worked for her.

What to Avoid: Avoid sounding as if you do not know how to handle difficult clients or as if your people skills are undeveloped.

59. What elements make a work environment positive?

What They Are Looking For: The interviewer is interested to hear you articulate the attributes you are seeking in a work environment. When you choose attributes to highlight in your response, consider what elements characterize the interviewing company's environment.

Sample Answer: "To me, the elements that make a positive work environment include talented colleagues, an atmosphere of collaboration and cooperation, a commitment to innovative ideas, and an honest atmosphere. In my experience, when those elements are present, employees are happy and willing to work harder. Wherever I am working, I try to help create and reinforce that sort of environment."

Analysis of Answer: The candidate outlines elements that many people would agree make a good work environment. By referring to her efforts to help create this sort of environment, the candidate gives a positive impression.

What to Avoid: Avoid naming characteristics that the interviewing organization lacks. If you do this, you will indicate that the job or interviewing organization is not ideal for you.

60. What have you done to make your current work environment more of a positive place to work?

What They Are Looking For: The interviewer is interested to hear how proactive you are as an employee and to what degree your unique presence makes your work environment a more pleasing place.

Sample Answer: "I have done several things to make my work environment more positive. On a team basis, I have helped to organize get-togethers outside of work, so as to build morale and camaraderie. On an officewide basis, I have helped initiate a mentoring program between the more senior employees and the new employees. This has helped people in the office get to know each other and made the workplace a much more closely knit environment."

Analysis of Answer: The candidate comes across as proactive in helping to make her work environment positive. Therefore, the candidate establishes a positive impression.

What to Avoid: Avoid sounding as if you do nothing to make the workplace a better environment. For small companies or organizations, your perceived willingness to help shape the work environment positively may be particularly important.

61. In your experience, what elements make for an excellent team member?

What They Are Looking For: Through this question the interviewer can assess what you value in other team members and what positive traits you have demonstrated yourself as a team member. This question gives you a chance to elaborate on qualities you associate with high-performing teams and to refer to an instance when you displayed those qualities. If you briefly refer to your experience, you can underscore the breadth of the experience you have gained—experience that can help you succeed in your new job.

Sample Answer: "Several attributes characterize an excellent team member. For instance, there is commitment to teamwork—that is, each member's willingness to play his or her role well, as well as to help others on the team as needed. Another attribute of an excellent team member is a willingness to work hard. Finally, the best team members usually possess a passion for new ideas that help the team keep its work sharp and innovative."

Analysis of Answer: The candidate does a good job of articulating many facets of an excellent team member. The candidate could have made this a better answer by referring to his own performance briefly, citing an example of his own excellent team participation.

What to Avoid: Avoid seeming as if you don't know what makes a good team member. If you are unfamiliar with these attributes, it implies you have not demonstrated them yourself in your teamwork.

62. Under what conditions would you fire someone?

What They Are Looking For: The interviewer is seeking to see what sort of manager you are. You may wish to give an answer that falls within the extremes of appearing to fire people quickly and being fearful of firing anyone. You might let the interviewer know that you are not quick to fire anyone except in the instance of a huge ethical or legal breach on the employee's part, and that you seek to help low-performing workers address their weaknesses. However, you should probably also indicate that, if necessary, you would consider terminating an underperforming professional who failed to improve his or her performance after a long period.

Sample Answer: "Firing an employee is not something I would do lightly. For me to feel comfortable terminating someone's employment, I would require of myself that I had communicated to that employee on at least three occasions that the employee was underperforming significantly, and that I had taken steps to work with the employee to address the area of weakness. If the employee showed a lack of motivation to improve or if, after a longer period, the employee simply did not have the talents and skills required for the job, at that point I would take steps to either move the employee to a different position or terminate the employee."

Analysis of Answer: The candidate comes across as fair and even-handed; these are good attributes.

What to Avoid: Try to ensure that you do not seem quick to fire someone, except in instances such as when an employee has engaged in an act that represents a huge ethical or legal breach. But also do not appear to fear the act of firing an underperforming or unmotivated employee, because an effective leader must sometimes make difficult decisions.

QUESTIONS ABOUT YOUR CAREER PROGRESSION

63. Why were you at that particular job such a short time?

What They Are Looking For: Through this question, the interviewer seeks an assurance that you can be a stable, reliable employee who does not have problems maintaining a job. If there is a job at which you were employed for a brief period, explain why your employment there was so brief. Try to keep your tone positive.

Sample Answer: "In my first job, I joined a start-up company that was only a few months old. I greatly enjoyed the experience, because I was given significant responsibilities as a member of a five-person team. However, after our initial funding, we had difficulty securing additional funding, and by the sixth month of its existence, the company had to close its doors. Even though our company did not succeed, I learned a tremendous amount about entrepreneurial ventures and team management. I would look forward to serving at your company for a long while and to drawing on my experience."

Analysis of Answer: The candidate kept a positive tone and tried to present a convincing explanation of the short-term employment. The candidate also provided assurances that his or her interest is in securing a longer-term position. This candidate likely left a positive impression.

What to Avoid: Assuming the employer is seeking an employee who will stay for a long while, avoid coming across as a candidate who will leave a job on a whim.

64. You have moved jobs often in the past four years. What explains that?

What They Are Looking For: The interviewer wants assurance that you can be a stable, reliable employee who does not have problems maintaining a job.

Sample Answer: "During the years right after I completed college, I was testing the waters, trying to find out what field I was most passionate about. Although I worked at three different companies for short periods of time, my record of achievement at each job remained very high. I made significant contributions as I completed the work on assigned projects before moving on. As you can see, in my last job, I stayed much longer—for two years. I finally have found the area that I am passionate about, and I hope to bring the skills I have developed in my last job to the new position that you are offering. At your company, I see myself staying for a long while, because I have learned through my research that you offer both the professional career development and the cultural environment that I am seeking."

Analysis of Answer: The candidate kept a positive tone and presented a convincing explanation of his changes in employment. The candidate also provided assurances that his or her interest is in securing a longer-term position.

What to Avoid: Assuming the employer is seeking an employee who will stay for a long while, avoid coming across as a candidate who will leave the advertised job quickly.

65. You have been with only one firm during your entire work experience. Do you think you will have a hard time integrating into a new work environment?

What They Are Looking For: This question may be posed if you have worked for years at one institution alone. The interviewer is trying to assess whether you are too set in your ways to be an innovative, dynamic worker who is open to new ideas or new ways of doing things.

Sample Answer: "Yes, I was employed at only one company for over ten years, but the wealth of knowledge I have attained and the diversity of my experiences there mean I will be able to integrate well into your new environment. I was fortunate to be engaged in innovative projects, which means I was often on the leading edge of new developments in the field. Also, I often worked directly with partner companies or client companies. Because I had to work closely with teams from those companies, I was exposed to other ways of conducting business and other business cultures. All of this means that I am adaptable and open to new ways of doing things."

Analysis of Answer: The candidate's response informs the interviewer that although the candidate was with one company for a long time, he was constantly engaged in innovative projects or in work with parties outside of that company. This suggests that the candidate is adaptable and open to new ways of doing things.

What to Avoid: Avoid sounding apologetic about a long tenure with one company. Present it as an asset instead, and highlight the diversity of your experience if possible.

QUESTIONS ABOUT LOSING OR LEAVING YOUR JOB

66. Did you leave your last job voluntarily?

What They Are Looking For: The interviewer is probing to find out if there was a problem with your performance in your last job. Assuming that you were not fired, you should respond to this question in a nondefensive manner, answering yes and then pointing out the reasons why you chose to leave your last job. Also mention the positive reasons why you are seeking employment with the interviewing company.

Sample Answer: "Yes, I chose to leave my job voluntarily. I had come to a natural point in my career when I had to make a decision about whether I would continue as a research analyst or seek to move my career in a different direction, becoming a policy maker instead. There are benefits to both types of work, but the main factor that inspired me to leave my job was the passion I felt for policy-making work whenever I had the opportunity to participate on policy teams. In particular, I loved the process of assessing current challenges and comparing effective solutions from across the country. I also loved the collaboration. I know that your organization focuses primarily on collaboration, teamwork, and current issues and has a strong voice in the policy-making world. Because I have a passion for this work, have research experience, and work well in teams, I believe there is a wonderful fit between what your organization needs in its new hire and what I offer."

Analysis of Answer: This answer is not defensive. It offers a believable explanation of why this is a good time for the candidate to change jobs and an explanation of why the interviewing organization offers an ideal opportunity. The candidate also provides details about the relevance of his or her experience and skills. The response should be well received.

What to Avoid: Avoid sounding defensive, and avoid seeming to lack a good reason for switching jobs. Try to sound directed and purposeful in your choices.

67. Why were you terminated?

What They Are Looking For: This question can be difficult to answer. Be careful how you phrase your response, and try not to unnecessarily undercut your skills and work experience when discussing why you were terminated.

Sample Answer: "Unfortunately, given the downturn of the telecommunications industry, my company had to make the difficult decision to cut 30 percent of its workforce. The decisions were not performance based, but based on a particular area of work. The service lines they decided to streamline were areas in which whole divisions of workers were laid off. I am happy for the time I served with my company, as it was a positive work environment and I was able to accomplish many of the goals I set—from developing excellent teamwork skills to working a great deal with customers. While I am sorry that my position was cut due to economic factors, I am prepared to make positive contributions in a new environment. I intend to draw on the skills and experiences of my last four years."

Analysis of Answer: The answer is upbeat and forthcoming, and it does not sound defensive. The tone of the answer will likely elicit a positive response from the interviewer. The candidate does a great job of making her time at the telecommunications company seem well spent and of projecting herself as someone who is goal oriented and has achieved her goals in spite of the eventual layoff. The candidate gives the interviewer a positive impression of the skills and attributes she can bring to the new job.

What to Avoid: Avoid sounding defensive or as if you are hiding something. Try to avoid sounding as if your experience at your prior company was wholly negative or a waste of time, unless there is a clear reason to present your time that way.

68. Why should this firm take a risk on you, given that you were fired from your last position?

What They Are Looking For: The interviewer wants assurance that you do not have major personality or work-related flaws that will prevent you from performing well at his or her organization. If you were fired, carefully phrase why you were terminated, trying not to unnecessarily undercut your skills and work experience as you give your answer. Emphasize the many successful elements of your overall record, and underscore the attributes and skills you bring that can help you perform excellently in your new position.

Sample Answer: "My termination from my prior position was not performance based. Unfortunately, given the downturn of the telecommunications industry, my company had to make the difficult decision to cut 30 percent of its workforce. I am happy for the time I served with my company, as it was a positive work environment and I was able to accomplish many of the goals I set—from developing excellent teamwork skills to working a great deal with the marketing department. Given the experiences and skills I picked up, I am prepared to make positive contributions in a new environment. When working for your company, I will be able to put to use the many leadership skills I developed as I managed multiple projects. I will also be able to draw on the many insights I gained from working so closely with our marketing department. With those skills and insights, I will enhance the marketing work at your company."

Analysis of Answer: The answer is upbeat and forthcoming and does not sound defensive. The candidate does a great job of making the time at the telecommunications company seem well spent and of projecting an image of someone who is goal oriented. The candidate underscores the key skills and insights that he can draw on in the new job.

What to Avoid: Avoid sounding defensive. Avoid sounding as if you have major personality or work-related flaws that will prevent you from excelling in the new work environment. Try to shift the focus quickly to your many accomplishments and the skills and experiences you can bring to bear in your new position.

OTHER DIFFICULT QUESTIONS

69. Tell me about your greatest professional failure.

What They Are Looking For: The interviewer is seeking to determine how you respond to failure as well as to learn whether you have made any significant mistake that might affect negatively his or her decision to hire you. Contrary to popular belief, this question provides you a great opportunity to pinpoint some positive attributes about yourself. Choose a professional example in which you fell short of a goal, but one that was not a major failure. Ideally, you will indicate what you learned from the failure and how you later put that knowledge to work, yielding many successes. If possible, elaborate briefly on an example of a success that flowed from the lessons you learned from that failure.

Sample Answer: "When I first began to manage a team, I was given a time-sensitive project with a very tight deadline. I believed that we would need seven days to complete the project. But I failed to consider that some of our work depended on another department, which had to deliver critical information to us. I did not keep close tabs on the other department's work, and I assumed they would deliver the information as planned. They did not. As a result, our work was set back by days. We had to work late hours, sometimes until two o'clock in the morning, to finish the project on schedule. I learned from this experience how important time management and communication are.

"Ever since that time, I have been conservative in my time projections, and I take into account major areas in which our work could be set back. If I am relying on work from an external group, I am certain to stay abreast of that group's work flow. As a result of my early failure, therefore, I learned to be excellent at time management and communication."

Analysis of Answer: This answer presents a failure that might be seen as a common mistake for a professional who is new to managing a project. It is therefore a relatively safe choice. The candidate explained her early failure concisely before moving on to underscore the lessons the candidate learned from the experience. The candidate successfully explains how the lessons became a resource as she moved on to manage other projects successfully.

What to Avoid: Avoid providing an example that represents a huge mistake that few professionals would have made. Also avoid choosing an example so recent that you cannot elaborate on how you have put the lessons you have learned to good use.

70. What explains this D on your transcript?

What They Are Looking For: With this question, if there is only one poor grade on your transcript, the interviewer is probably looking for a brief explanation. We all go through hard circumstances, so an interviewer can understand if you went through some circumstance that resulted in a poor grade. If you have only one poor grade or a few that are concentrated in a particular period of time, you might wish to emphasize the difficult circumstances you were experiencing and then point to the many successes you have experienced since that time.

Sample Answer: "During the second semester of my junior year, I had to increase the number of hours I spent working in my part-time job because my parents were not able to assist me that semester with my living expenses. The course in mathematics in which I did not do well was very time-intensive and competitive. Devoting twenty hours a week to my part-time job meant I had less time available for studying, and that single grade reflects this. You will notice that there is no other poor grade on my record and that I fared well in all other math courses I took. That one poor grade is a result of very specific circumstances and does not reflect my math abilities. The other courses on my transcript, such as calculus and statistics, are much better indicators of my abilities."

Analysis of Answer: This answer provides a believable explanation for the poor grade—the need to work while in school. The answer also points to other indications of success in the candidate's record.

What to Avoid: Avoid explanations that draw on personal circumstances such as a romantic relationship as a reason for a poor grade. Also, avoid explanations that present you as irresponsible, such as saying you attended too many parties that semester. The interviewer will want to believe that you are able to keep your personal matters from impinging upon your work.

71. Your college grades in math were quite low. Even though this is a speech-writing job, do you feel those low grades are something we should be concerned about?

What They Are Looking For: The interviewer is probably concerned about a trend that appears on your transcript. Many of us are stronger in some subjects than in others. Through this question, the interviewer is asking about low grades concentrated in a subject that is not very relevant to the job for which you are applying. In this situation, keep your response brief, noting that you are not strong in that particular subject but emphasizing how strong your grades are in other subjects that are more relevant to the job you are seeking to attain.

Sample Answer: "Ever since I was young, I have shown a clear strength in my writing and communication abilities, whereas I have received only average grades in math. During college, we were required to take three math courses, and those lower grades reflect the fact that I have never been strong in math. The job I am interviewing for today centers on speech writing and calls for strong skills in writing and communication. You can see from my transcript that I excelled in those areas. My GPA in my major of English is very high. Likewise, I won two awards for my writing during college. I am hoping that my record of success in areas that are critical for this job—writing and communication—will be the basis of my selection for the position you are offering."

Analysis of Answer: The candidate does a good job of acknowledging the poor grades in a nondefensive manner and then shifting the focus quickly to his strengths in the areas that are important for the job for which he is interviewing. The candidate proceeds to outline specific indicators of success—from the high GPA to the awards—in the areas that are most relevant to the job.

What to Avoid: Do not fail to acknowledge the poor grades if you have several, but try to shift the focus to your strengths and your qualifications for the job.

72. This job focuses a great deal on finance. I notice your college grades in math were quite low. Do you have an explanation? We are very concerned about this.

What They Are Looking For: The interviewer is probably concerned about a trend that appears on your transcript. If your grades are low in an area that is related to the job for which you are interviewing, you are best off providing other indicators of your success in that subject matter. For instance, perhaps you took courses after college and did well in that same subject matter. Or perhaps your standardized-test scores in that arena are strong. Acknowledge the poor trend on your transcript, but then offer the other indicators as better measurements of your abilities.

Sample Answer: "I realize that math is very important for the job you are offering. For some reason, I had a difficult time learning math well during college. It might have been because of the overall demands of my schedule or the demand of working part-time. But understanding how important this subject is to my future, I have taken steps to strengthen my math skills. I enrolled in four specialized courses during the summer after my college graduation, and I maintained a high grade point average in those courses. I went on to take several standardized tests as I prepared to attain a one-year master's degree, and you can see from those scores that my math score ranked above the 90th percentile. In my current job, I have employed my strong math skills in financial modeling. My successes since college demonstrate that performance in math is now a strength, not a weakness, in my performance."

Analysis of Answer: The candidate does not make light of the poor record. The candidate presents the image of someone who has made sure to address a weakness that is relevant to the available job by taking specialized courses and redoubling his efforts to strengthen skills in that area. The candidate does a good job of pointing to indicators that attest to his strengthened skills in the critical area.

73. Your overall grades in college were quite low. What explains this?

What They Are Looking For: The interviewer is concerned that your low college grades indicate a lack of motivation, commitment, or intellectual ability. You are best off addressing this concern by pointing to other successes that demonstrate your motivation, commitment, and/or intellectual ability.

Sample Answer: "Yes, my college GPA was low. Unfortunately when I attended college, I suffered from youthful ignorance and was not at all focused on my studies. I focused on just about everything else—community projects, college extracurricular activities, and participation in college sports. In terms of serving as a strong leader on campus and helping to contribute to campus life, I would receive an A. But I recognize now the poor judgment in my choice to neglect my studies. I cannot turn back the clock, but I have taken significant steps to make up for the lost opportunity to excel in my college studies. I have enrolled in many extension classes at the local college, where I have maintained an A average in courses relevant to this job, such as marketing. I have also taken the opportunity to become certified in computing, since I seek to blend my business and technology skills. I have also attained a very high record of success in my career, with two promotions in the last three years. I am hoping that my record of success since college will assure you of my ability to excel in the job you are offering."

Analysis of Answer: The answer does a good job of acknowledging the poor college record in an even-toned way. The candidate does not make light of the poor record. Nor does the candidate make excuses for the poor record. The candidate presents the image of someone who has recognized an error in judgment and taken the initiative to develop a better record. The interviewer will likely see this response in a positive light.

What to Avoid: Avoid appearing to make light of your poor record, if you have a poor record to explain. Take responsibility for the poor record, but emphasize what you have done since that time to strengthen your record of achievement and skills.

PERSONAL QUESTIONS

74. Why do you want to work in this city?

What They Are Looking For: The interviewer is interested in hearing you express a sincere interest in the city, which indicates that you might want to stay in that city—particularly if it is a new city for you—for some time. It is a good idea to have a sense of the benefits the city offers so that you can reference these benefits in your response. If you have friends or family in the area, you might also mention this, to further indicate the depth of your interest in the city.

Sample Answer: "I am attracted to Boston for many reasons. I see Boston as a city in which my career can grow, especially given the strong base of business that exists in the region. Boston's expanding base of medium-sized business ventures is attractive. There are also more personal reasons why I want to work in Boston. I attended college here, and my ties to the community are deep—both in terms of my friendships with former classmates who are now businesspeople in this region and in terms of my ties to community organizations. I have always enjoyed Boston, given its history and culture, and the many areas of town to enjoy such as downtown, the harbor, and Newton. Also, Boston offers communities in which I would enjoy living again and in which I can envision raising a family."

Analysis of Answer: This answer does a good job of highlighting an array of reasons why Boston is an ideal choice for the candidate. The candidate makes sure to touch on the professional aspects that make the city attractive. The candidate also adds a personal touch to the reasons, with references to friends and community organizations.

What to Avoid: Assuming you believe the company is seeking a longer-term employee, avoid sounding as if you have not thought deeply about whether the city is attractive for the long term. Also avoid sounding as if you have not considered a wide array of reasons why the city is an attractive place to live and work.

75. What do you do outside of work?

What They Are Looking For: The reasons why an interviewer might ask this question can vary. In general, you should seek to demonstrate that you are not "all work and no play." People like to work with people they find interesting. Focus your answer on activities that show a depth to your personality and diversity in your interests and that also underscore some of your winning qualities, such as intellectual curiosity, desire to help others, or teamwork.

Sample Answer: "My work is very demanding, so I have little personal time in this phase of my career. However, with the time I do have, I make sure to devote time to community service through a group called Community Action. I serve on a committee that convenes once every three weeks to provide valuable services at various boys' and girls' clubs. We help to teach arts and sports. It has been wonderful to keep that part of my life active in spite of my long work hours."

Analysis of Answer: This answer demonstrates that the candidate seeks a balanced life and places a positive value on participating in activities within communities. This reflects well on the candidate's potential attitude toward company activities. The interviewer is likely to believe this candidate will help keep the workplace pleasant.

What to Avoid: While the degree to which companies value extracurricular activities varies widely, it is a good idea to have some type of activity to mention so that you do not appear to lack a lighter side to your personality.

76. How do you seek to balance work and home life?

What They Are Looking For: The reasons why an interviewer might ask this question can vary widely, but in most cases the interviewer is probing to see whether the balance you try to keep between work and home responsibilities is consistent with the demands of the job for which you are interviewing. If the organization you are trying to work for is very family oriented, you should probably underscore your commitment to hard work and family values. If the organization you want to work for is known for working employees hard and expects employees to make significant sacrifices with regard to family, you may want to answer in a way that clarifies your willingness to put in long hours if needed.

Sample Answer: "At this phase of my banking career, my time is in great demand professionally. It has been a challenge to maintain a balance. My wife also works in a highly demanding job, so we have decided to carve out time with each other in the mornings rather than in the evenings. Often, we cannot control whether we must work until ten o'clock at night, and we are very tired when we get home. So we have reoriented our time to get up an hour earlier each day and spend time together over breakfast or working out. We also try to carve out time together on our weekends. This has helped me maintain balance."

Analysis of Answer: This is a wonderful response in an instance when the available job is known to be very time-intensive and demanding. The candidate demonstrates that he accepts the high demands of his work without much complaint, and that he has found a creative way to balance those demands against the desire to maintain a good social and family life. This answer would not likely make the interviewer nervous that a high-demand job would be incompatible with the desired lifestyle of the candidate.

What to Avoid: Avoid an answer that sounds as if you are whining about your work hours or that might make the interviewer nervous that the demands of the job you are applying for would be incompatible with your lifestyle.

77. Whom do you most admire?

What They Are Looking For: By indicating whom you most admire, you also indicate the types of achievements and traits you admire. The interviewer is interested to hear about this, because it reflects your values and attributes. Choose a person, therefore, who reflects attributes and values that will also reflect well on you.

Sample Answer: "I most admire Martin Kingmaker, a highly successful local businessman, for a number of reasons. I admire the fact that he followed his passion. I have met many professionals who regret that when the opportunity arose, they did not pursue a career in which they could follow their passions. I also admire Mr. Kingmaker's vision and the fact that he was able to translate that vision into a notable success. That took diligence, discipline, and hard work. Equally important, I admire his commitment to employing professionals from a wide range of backgrounds. His employees represent a wide range of countries and ethnicities. His choices and achievements represent qualities I try to develop in myself."

Analysis of Answer: This answer does a wonderful job of explaining clearly why the candidate admires the local businessperson. It also is a good response because the local businessman possesses many admirable traits and the job candidate draws a parallel to his own attributes as he closes his response.

What to Avoid: Avoid sounding as if you admire someone only because of the person's fame, wealth, or power. At times, those values can be seen as negatives if you do not mention other attributes such as the person's hard work, community contributions, or ethics.

78. What is one of your defining experiences?

What They Are Looking For: The interviewer uses this question to understand what motivates you. If the interviewer asks you to recount a defining experience, you have a wonderful opportunity to carve an answer that highlights the winning attributes that have helped you attain many successes in your life. For instance, suppose you failed an exam in junior high school but used the experience to develop both a strong vision of your future and the determination to try harder and excel in that same subject. You can use this question as a chance to elaborate a theme about yourself: You became someone with strong vision and determination. From there, talk about the many wonderful successes you have experienced.

Sample Answer: "I am motivated by a deep desire to help produce new products that will help make life easier for people around the world. This motivation developed as a result of one of my defining experiences—the hardship I experienced one summer when living in rural Chile, where excellent products are hard to come by. It was very different from England. After that difficult summer, I immigrated to the United States with my parents. I was twelve. But the hardships I had seen in Chile inspired me to take the opportunity to develop my skills so that when I went to college, I could train to become an engineer. That summer in Chile continues to motivate me as I design affordable home care products that will be ideal in developing countries and can help ease the burden of everyday activities for many people around the world. Your company's commitment to this same goal is one of the biggest reasons why I am seeking a job with your company."

Analysis of Answer: This answer is good because it pinpoints a defining experience and links the development of the candidate's motivation to that experience. The candidate also does an excellent job of using this as a basis for demonstrating compatibility with the goals of the interviewing company.

What to Avoid: Avoid elaborating on an experience that does not help highlight your winning traits.

79. What early experiences led you on your current career track?

What They Are Looking For: The interviewer is using this question to understand what motivates you. If the interviewer asks you about the early experiences that have led to your current career path, take the opportunity to elaborate on sources of motivation that present you in an excellent light. For instance, you can mention how your early experiences in school instilled in you a love of learning and innovation, which spurred you to explore a career with those characteristics. As you anwer this question, you can demonstrate a wonderful fit with the interviewing organization.

Sample Answer: "I am motivated by a deep desire to help improve education through technology. This interest stems from my own upbringing in the inner city of Chicago, where technological tools were hard to come by. However, in today's business world, companies see the benefits of extending computer literacy to all parts of the country, and since many inner-city schools have become Internet accessible, there is now a tremendous opportunity to improve education through technology. Seeing these trends, I chose to major in computer science while I was in college, and I sought a job after graduation with a small technology company that was known for innovative products. I had a wonderful two years in my first job, and now I am ready to apply my knowledge of educational IT tools in a larger company whose sole focus lies in this area. Your company is ideal, given its focus and its commitment to deploying excellent technology throughout school systems in upper- as well as lower-income areas."

Analysis of Answer: This answer is good because it pinpoints a concrete set of early experiences that sparked the candidate's deep interest. The candidate then links that interest to her career ambitions. The candidate does an excellent job of using this as a basis for demonstrating compatibility with the goals of the interviewing company.

What to Avoid: Avoid using this question to elaborate on early experiences that had no role in developing your winning traits.

80. What is your favorite hobby?

What They Are Looking For: The reasons why an interviewer might ask this question can vary. In general, you should seek to demonstrate you are not "all work and no play." If the interviewer asks you about your favorite hobby, you have a wonderful chance to relate key information about attributes that will make you an excellent employee. Choose a hobby at which you have excelled and that demonstrates your favorable characteristics. Don't underestimate any hobby you have. Think about what you love about it, and be able to articulate how it enriches you and the people around you.

Sample Answer: "I really enjoy playing soccer in a local community league. What I enjoy most about playing soccer is the way I have to focus on attaining goals and the way in which I have to play an effective role on a team in order to attain success. Besides that, it is just good fun and enables me to remain fit."

Analysis of Answer: This answer stresses qualities about the game that are relevant in the business world—playing a good role in a team and focusing to attain a goal. The candidate uses his response to reinforce a positive image.

What to Avoid: Avoid mentioning a hobby that might not be seen in a positive light.

81. What is your favorite extracurricular activity?

What They Are Looking For: The reasons why an interviewer might ask a student this question can vary, but many interviewers use this question to assess a fit between the attributes you highlight through your response and the attributes of an ideal candidate for the job. If the interview asks you about your favorite extracurricular activity, you have a great chance to focus on the winning attributes that will make you an excellent employee. Choose an activity that demonstrates characteristics the interviewer will value, such as teamwork, a commitment to improving your school's or community's environment, or a commitment to helping others gain greater knowledge.

Sample Answer: "I really enjoy working for the Campus Volunteer Leadership Association as an extracurricular activity. We help provide student leaders for various charitable projects in our community based on the students' interests and skills. I enjoy that work because it allows me to contribute to my community, as well as to meet other students who are seeking to make positive contributions. This activity fits well with my values. I have already helped organize teams that have completed multiple projects. It has been a fun opportunity to employ my organizational and leadership skills while also giving back to the community."

Analysis of Answer: This answer stresses several appealing qualities of the extracurricular activity: making a contribution to the community, organizing students, and using leadership skills. The candidate therefore reinforces a positive image.

What to Avoid: Avoid elaborating on an extracurricular activity that might not be seen in a positive light. When possible, choose something that highlights business-relevant attributes or skills.

PERSONALITY QUESTIONS

82. How would you describe yourself?

What They Are Looking For: This is an open-ended question, and the interviewer will assess how articulate your response is as well as whether the characteristics you highlight are ideal for the available job. You can answer it in much the same way that you might have responded to the query "Tell me about yourself." Use memorable adjectives that reinforce the qualities and skills the interviewer will value, and elaborate if possible with reference to specific achievements.

Sample Answer: "I am hardworking, directed, and interested in people from different places. Those attributes helped me excel in college. These attributes have also served me well in my company, since it is a diverse multinational company with projects that often involve work in multiple countries. I have enjoyed working on projects with teams from countries such as South Africa and Mexico. My hard work has enabled me to bring success to our clients, and my direction has helped me inspire confidence in my superiors, who promoted me last year to assistant manager. Because your company is multinational and focused on work that requires directed and focused professionals, I believe I will blend in well here."

Analysis of Answer: The answer centers on attributes that immediately paint the candidate as an interesting and perhaps ideal choice for a company. The candidate emphasizes a good fit with the company.

What to Avoid: Avoid mentioning attributes that do not demonstrate a match or that do not show your ability to flourish in the available job. If you refer to some of your achievements, try to use a modest tone (don't come across as bragging too much).

83. Name three adjectives that describe you.

What They Are Looking For: The interviewer is looking for a match between the qualities needed in an ideal job candidate and the way you describe yourself. With this in mind, describe yourself using adjectives that reinforce qualities and skills the interviewer will value. If possible, elaborate with reference to specific achievements.

Sample Answer: "I am analytical, creative, and hardworking. I have served on many teams in which my analyses were pivotal to the overall success of our team. As a result, my supervisors have given me increasing responsibilities at work. I also have a natural tendency to consider new solutions to problems, thinking about how to use best practices in other fields in ways that are relevant to the telecommunications industry. Finally, my willingness to work hard has helped drive my success both in school, where I held a high GPA, and at work."

Analysis of Answer: The answer is concise and focuses on attributes that are relevant to the professional environment. This answer can help the interviewer conclude that the candidate is a good choice for the available job.

What to Avoid: Avoid mentioning attributes that do not highlight your strengths. Focus on traits that demonstrate a fit with the available job.

84. What is your greatest weakness?

What They Are Looking For: Overall, the interviewer is looking for a match between the qualities of an ideal job candidate and your qualities. Therefore, when speaking of a weakness, the weakness you mention should not be in one of the areas in which you must demonstrate a strength in order to succeed in the available job. Use caution when choosing a weakness to elaborate on.

Sample Answer: "My greatest weakness is a tendency to be too detail oriented. There are times when work in our industry must be done quickly and solving 80 percent of the problem is more than sufficient for meeting our goals. If I try to attain perfection, I could waste a great deal of time. So, I constantly try to delineate my goals to make sure I am not putting in too much time on a project or doing unnecessary work."

Analysis of Answer: This is a common weakness, so mentioning this is not likely to hurt the candidate much in the interviewing process. The candidate was careful to indicate an effort to address the weakness, which the interviewer will see as a constructive reaction to a weakness.

What to Avoid: Avoid mentioning a weakness that puts into question your ability to excel in the job for which you are applying.

85. What is your greatest strength?

What They Are Looking For: The interviewer is looking for a match between the qualities needed in an ideal job candidate and the way you describe your greatest strength. Choose a strength that reinforces the qualities and skills the interviewer will value. If possible, elaborate with reference to specific achievements.

Sample Answer: "My greatest strength is my ability to work well with others. This made me an excellent team participant, when I needed to assist others with difficult situations. This also enabled me to be a great team leader, because I needed to get to know my team members well in order to manage them excellently. Finally, my ability to work well with others means I am good with our clients, which is always a plus for advancing in this career field. One of the reasons I would look forward to the chance to work for your company as a project manager is that I will be able to put my strength to use as I manage large teams and help attract new business."

Analysis of Answer: This answer is wonderful in mentioning a strength that reinforces the skills the candidate needs to succeed in the available job.

What to Avoid: Avoid mentioning a strength that is not relevant at all to your ability to excel in the job for which you are applying. Take the opportunity to use this question to underscore your winning attributes and qualifications for the job.

86. What motivates you?

What They Are Looking For: In seeking to understand what motivates you, the interviewer can probe to see if your passion or goals are suitable given the available job. This is a very open-ended question that provides an opportunity for you to use your motivations as a way to tout your major achievements and strengths. Motivations can vary from "a passion for learning," to "a love of serving others." Once you offer a motivation or two, elaborate with specifics about the successes you have achieved as a result of your motivation.

Sample Answer: "I am motivated by a deep desire to help others through innovative medical products. This motivation developed when I was in junior high school, when I lost one of my favorite aunts to cancer. It was difficult watching her health deteriorate and sensing the helplessness of the doctors. That sparked my interest in sciences, and I soon began to excel in the sciences. This interest stayed with me throughout college, and the more I explored the companies devoted to developing new medical devices, the more I understood I wanted to dedicate my life to working for such a company."

Analysis of Answer: This answer is good because it explains the candidate's motivation and elaborates on a believable reason why the candidate has that motivation. This particular response may also be attractive to an interviewer because the candidate implies that her interest in the field is long-standing and firm.

What to Avoid: Avoid elaborating on motivations that might be perceived as highly negative.

87. How would your friends describe you?

What They Are Looking For: The interviewer is looking for a match between the qualities you highlight and the qualities of the ideal job candidate. This is an open-ended question that enables you to focus immediately on the winning attributes and skills you need to excel in your potential new work environment. Take the opportunity to direct the conversation toward strengths that the interviewing organization will find most attractive.

Sample Answer: "My friends would describe me as very directed and excellent at setting goals. They would point to my strong record in college as an example of my ability to be directed and to excel in a competitive environment. They would also look at my promotions in my current job as evidence of my goal-setting tendencies. In spite of my hard work and drive, though, my friends would also say I am a lot of fun to be around. I try to keep balance in my life by continuing to work in the community in my spare time and by participating in outdoor activities such as hiking and biking with my friends."

Analysis of Answer: The candidate focuses centrally on attributes and the aspects of his record that will be appealing to the interviewer—hard work and goal orientation. The candidate also makes sure to mention being fun, since it is the candidate's friends who are supposed to be commenting. This response paints the candidate in a positive light.

What to Avoid: Avoid focusing on attributes that do not shed much light on your ability to perform in the position for which you are applying or that create the image of someone who would be dull or boring to work with.

88. How would your teammates describe you?

What They Are Looking For: The interviewer is looking for a match between the attributes you highlight and the attributes of the ideal candidate. This is an open-ended question that enables you to focus immediately on the winning attributes and skills you need to excel in your potential new work environment. Take the opportunity to direct the conversation toward strengths that the interviewing organization will find most attractive. Because the question is about team members, be certain to touch on qualities that make for an excellent team member or team leader.

Sample Answer: "My team members would describe me as cooperative, insightful, and creative. They think of me as cooperative because they remember the times that I helped them solve problems they faced, even though the matter might not have been my particular responsibility. They would say I am insightful because they would remember how many times my analysis helped to shed light on our projects. They would say I was creative because I am known for innovative thinking. Those attributes make me an excellent team member."

Analysis of Answer: The answer is concise and focuses on attributes associated with good team participation. This response paints the candidate in a positive light.

What to Avoid: Avoid focusing on attributes that do not shed much light on your ability to perform well as a team member.

89. How would your supervisor describe you?

What They Are Looking For: The interviewer is looking for a match between the traits you highlight and the traits your supervisors at the interviewing company would hope to find in the ideal job candidate. This is an open-ended question that enables you to center your answer on the positive attributes and capabilities that can help you perform excellently in the available job. Because the response should reflect what your supervisor thinks of you, tailor your wording to reflect qualities of particular value to a supervisor.

Sample Answer: "My superior would describe me as directed, excellent at setting goals, and creative. Another of my goals has been to consistently deliver excellent work on the job. Another thing that has meant a great deal to me is to consistently perform successfully at work. I have done this by ensuring I understood the goal of all projects I have led and by meeting with all of the key parties to a project to make sure we were all aligned in our objectives. I have also attained excellence by leading my teams to develop creative solutions for our clients. I motivate my teams to think outside of the box. My ability to perform so well in my current job provides the basis of my ability to do well in the managerial position you are offering."

Analysis of Answer: The candidate focuses on attributes and the aspects of his or her record that are most meaningful to the interviewer. Her response concludes well as the candidate points out that her record of success provides a basis for future success as a manager.

What to Avoid: Avoid focusing on attributes that do not shed much light on your ability to perform excellently in the position for which you are applying.

90. If two managers were discussing you, what would they be saying?

What They Are Looking For: Just as in Question 89, through this question the interviewer is looking for a match between the traits and accomplishments you highlight and the traits and accomplishments of the ideal job candidate. Emphasize the key attributes that will make you an excellent choice for the new job.

Sample Answer: "If two managers were discussing me, they would focus on my record of success and the consistency of my performance. One of my personal goals has been to perform with consistent success at work. I do this by ensuring I understand the goals of all projects I have led and by meeting with all of the key parties to a project to make sure we were all aligned in our objectives. I have also managed teams well by focusing our efforts carefully and prioritizing in ways that ensure we deliver work on schedule. My ability to perform so well provides the basis of my ability to do well in the managerial position you are offering."

Analysis of Answer: The candidate focuses on aspects of her record that are most meaningful to the company conducting the interview. The candidate closes her response well as she points out that her record of success provides a basis for future success as a manager.

What to Avoid: Avoid focusing on attributes that do not shed much light on your ability to perform excellently in the position for which you are applying.

91. How can your superiors most easily motivate you?

What They Are Looking For: The interviewer is asking you to comment on what sorts of incentives motivate you in the workplace. Perhaps affirm that you normally remain highly motivated without the need for extra prodding, but also mention other incentives that you react positively to, such as the chance to make a significant difference to the client.

Sample Answer: "I rarely need others to motivate me, as I am very directed in my own career and am the sort of person who enjoys taking the initiative. But if my superiors want to try to motivate me more, it would be by underscoring the importance of my work to our company and clients. It is important to me that my work is excellent and that

I make a difference through my work. When that is affirmed, it helps to inspire me."

Analysis of Answer: This answer is good because the candidate conveys self-motivation and self-direction. The response also emphasizes that the candidate places great value on providing excellent work for her company and clients. These are all pluses in the interview process.

What to Avoid: Avoid sounding as if you are difficult to motivate or as if you need constant motivation from your supervisors. In many situations, it is also risky to imply that your sole motivation is money.

92. Give me a recent example of constructive criticism you have received at work from a supervisor.

What They Are Looking For: The interviewer is asking you to state what one of your weaknesses is. Since they are asking you to reveal such information from the perspective of a superior, this can be a tricky question to answer. Be careful what you choose to speak about, because you want to preserve the notion that you are an excellently performing employee.

Sample Answer: "I recently received feedback that I should provide more critical evaluations of my junior associates. My supervisor reviewed my favorable comments about most of my team members during their latest review, and commented that my evaluations were not critical enough. My supervisor agrees that our team performed wonderfully as it developed excellent computing systems for multiple divisions of our company. But she points out that everyone has room for improvement. My evaluation style has been to provide critical feedback orally, and when I see my associates improve their weaknesses, I have chosen to minimize the written feedback about those weaknesses. I understand and accept my superior's criticism and have made a point to be more detailed in my written evaluations. If I were to begin to work with your computing systems company, I would seek to understand clearly what sort of feedback you would like me to provide about the people I supervise, because professional development is very important."

Analysis of Answer: This is a relatively harmless answer. It provides criticism about a particular area that is not likely to be seen as central to the skills needed to excel in the available computing job. The candidate balanced his response well by indicating the team he led had worked excellently in spite of his tendency to provide more feedback orally rather than in writing.

What to Avoid: Avoid discussing an area that will imply you are weak in skills, knowledge, or experience that is critical for success in your potential new job.

93. What makes you unique?

What They Are Looking For: The interviewer is seeking a match between the characteristics you highlight and the characteristics of an ideal candidate. The interviewer is offering you an open-ended question that lets you focus on the positive attributes and capabilities that can help you excel in your potential new work environment.

Sample Answer: "The diversity and depth of my work experience help to make me unique. I have lived in four different countries. I have enjoyed different cultures and enjoy getting to know the histories of exotic places. Fortunately, I have also had the opportunity to lead teams in each of those countries—in Egypt, England, Brazil, and the United States. As a result of those experiences, I have learned to work with multinational teams. This would be a big asset at your firm, because of your firm's diversity. I will be able to manage diverse teams well, which is needed in the job you are interviewing for."

Analysis of Answer: This answer focuses on one broad theme that supports the notions that this candidate is prepared to blend into the environment of the interviewing firm, and has a skill—managing diverse teams—that will enable him to succeed in his new job. The candidate could have also focused on two or three attributes, rather than the one broad theme of diversity.

What to Avoid: Avoid focusing for too long on attributes that are irrelevant to your professional career or the position for which you are applying.

94. What are your most memorable characteristics?

What They Are Looking For: The interviewer will assess whether there is a fit between the characteristics you highlight and the characteristics of an ideal candidate. This is an open-ended question. Center your reply on the key attributes that help make you a good choice for the new job.

Sample Answer: "My most memorable characteristics are creativity, hard work, and a friendly personality. My creativity can be seen as I helped launch a new club during college, which grew to be one of the largest health education clubs on campus by my senior year. My work with that health education club gave me a lot of leadership experience. My creativity can also be seen through my success in leading two innovative marketing campaigns at my current company. My hard work is evident through the success of my marketing campaigns. And my friendly personality has manifested itself both through my community work and through my team leadership. I know others enjoy working with me, which is one reason why my teams do so well. I believe my memorable characteristics will help me be an excellent marketing manager at your company."

Analysis of Answer: This answer does a good job of focusing on three attributes that are relevant to the candidate's ability to be an effective and pleasant professional to work with. The candidate does a good job of providing examples for each attribute she highlights and of using the opportunity to focus attention on achievements that make her qualified for a marketing position.

What to Avoid: Avoid focusing on attributes that are not relevant to the position you are applying for or that fail to paint you as a person with whom others would want to work.

95. Tell me about a trip you have enjoyed and what you liked most about it.

What They Are Looking For: If appropriate, make this answer deeper than simply "I liked that city because it has a lot of restaurants that stay open late." The interviewer is offering you an opportunity to stress attributes such as your enjoyment of different cultures, your appreciation of history, or your enjoyment of activities such as hiking or camping. Those choices can be seen as indicating a passion for diversity, intellectual curiosity, and a desire to challenge oneself, respectively. Those qualities make for a good worker. As such, they can serve as key parts of a good response. Carve your answer so that it reveals deeper qualities about your personality that indicate you will be an interesting colleague or a good worker.

Sample Answer: "I recently took a trip to Oklahoma and drove down through Arizona. I had the opportunity to visit several local Native American cultural centers and the Grand Canyon. I am intellectually curious, so those aspects of the trip were wonderful. I enjoyed learning more about the history of our country, as well as about the culture of Native Americans. I am also a nature lover; I spend a lot of my time outside of work on camping and hiking trips. So the opportunity to see so much of our country's natural beauty on this road trip was ideal for me. The Grand Canyon is spectacular. I really enjoyed seeing such a beautiful piece of America, and I hope to be able to visit again in the future."

Analysis of Answer: This answer was good because the candidate underscored his intellectual curiosity, love of learning about other cultures, and enjoyment of nature. This candidate succeeds in making the interviewer think that he or she will be an interesting person to have around, and highlights traits often found in a good worker.

What to Avoid: Avoid providing a bland answer that fails to reinforce a positive image of yourself. Instead, try to use this question to weave in extra bits of information that make you sound interesting and highlight the traits of a good worker.

96. If you could travel across the country with someone famous, who would it be, and why?

What They Are Looking For: The interviewer is looking for you to reveal deeper qualities about yourself through this answer. By revealing whom you might want to complete a cross-country drive with, you are presumably pointing out someone you admire. Thus, you are also commenting on attributes you hold in high esteem. Use this question as a way to underscore your own admirable qualities, if possible.

Sample Answer: "If I had the chance to travel across the country with someone famous, I would choose former South African President Nelson Mandela. There are lots of reasons why. First of all, I greatly admire his commitment to freedom and his willingness to pay a high price for what he felt was right. He exemplifies courage and high ethics. Second, I admire his ability to have a vision of a country in which people work together across differences in gender and ethnicity. That is a vision that much of the rest of the world is working toward. I would also like to have the chance to ask him how he managed to keep focused on his goals through so many hardships. I am someone who is very goal oriented and who is diligently pursuing a vision of my own future. I would have much to learn from Nelson Mandela."

Analysis of Answer: This answer is good because the candidate chooses someone that most people would agree is a notable, admirable figure. Likewise, the reasons the candidate offers for his admiration indicate that those characteristics—courage, high ethics, goal orientation—are characteristics he is trying to emulate. Therefore, this response presents the candidate in a positive light.

What to Avoid: Avoid choosing a highly controversial figure or a figure whom you admire based solely on factors such as money or fame, as you might miss an opportunity to underscore important values about yourself that are relevant to the job for which you are applying.

END-OF-INTERVIEW QUESTIONS

97. Where else are you interviewing?

What They Are Looking For: The interviewer wants a frank statement of the other organizations with which you are interviewing. If the interviewer asks you where else you are interviewing, be straightforward. Recruiters at companies in the same industry sometimes know each other, so you do not want to be less than forthcoming and have the interviewer discover that you omitted information or fudged your answers. But you can still restate and underscore your deep interest in the company with which you are interviewing.

Sample Answer: "I am interviewing with three pharmaceutical companies in this area. However, you are my top choice. As I mentioned, I have been looking for a company that is known for focusing on affordable, innovative health care products and medicine, and one that is particularly focused on elderly health care. Your specialization and the appealing corporate culture of this company are what makes me so attracted to this firm."

Analysis of Answer: This candidate does a good job of answering the question directly while underscoring why this company is the ideal one for him.

What to Avoid: Avoid sounding as if you are being less than forth-coming or omitting important information. Avoid sounding as if you are indifferent about which of the firms you will work for, if you are interviewing with other companies. Instead, underscore why the firm with which you are interviewing is ideal for you.

98. Do you have any questions about our company?

What They Are Looking For: The interviewer is normally interested in addressing questions you have. When interviewers ask you to pose questions about their company, err on the side of caution. In the interviewing phase, your goal is to land the job, so you do not want to ask any risky questions at this point. Remember, the interviewer will assess whether your questions indicate you are an ideal choice for the company. If possible, ask questions that help demonstrate a fit between you and the company. If possible, also ask questions that demonstrate you know the basics about the company.

Sample Answer: "I understand that, given the many challenges of the current environment, your consulting company has decided to launch a restructuring division to help companies adversely affected by the economic downturn. To my understanding, your company will help them streamline after they have filed for bankruptcy. That sounds like a valuable service to provide companies. Will other parts of your company, such as the corporate consulting division, be able to share lessons learned from your restructuring work in order to assist other companies that are also distressed but not in bankruptcy? I am curious about how you share best practices throughout the firm."

Analysis of Answer: This question should be addressed to an interviewer who has knowledge of the practices within this company. The question demonstrates that the candidate has done his or her homework and is aware of the company's new initiative to establish a restructuring division. Asking how the company leverages its knowledge across its divisions is good because the candidate shows general curiosity about how to deliver excellence to clients.

What to Avoid: Avoid questions that paint you in a bad light, such as too much concern about salary levels. Such questions are normally best asked after the job has been offered to you. Do not ask questions that demonstrate you lack basic knowledge about the company.

99. What additional questions can I answer for you?

What They Are Looking For: The interviewer wants to answer your questions but will also be listening to hear whether your questions indicate a fit or lack of fit with the company or job. If the interviewer invites you to pose questions, stay with simple questions that have fairly predictable answers. Your goal in the interviewing phase is to land the job, so err on the side of caution. If possible, ask questions that help demonstrate a fit between you and the company. Also ask knowledge-able questions to demonstrate you have done your homework about the job, the team with which you might work, and the company.

Sample Answer: "When reading through current business articles, I was interested to learn that, partly thanks to your corporate culture that encourages innovation, this company has doubled its client base and is seeking to expand its Houston base in the area of gas and energy consulting. What have you most enjoyed about the work in this area?"

Analysis of Answer: This question should be addressed to an interviewer who works in the gas or energy practice. This question conveys to the interviewer that the candidate has done her homework and is familiar with the direction the company is taking. The question also asks the interviewer to comment about a personal experience, which will likely create a positive reaction.

What to Avoid: Avoid sounding as if you do not know the basics about the company or industry, or as if you have not completed your homework about the available job and the individuals with whom you might be working.

100. Is there anything else you'd like to tell me before we conclude this interview?

What They Are Looking For: The interviewer is offering you the opportunity to recap the themes you had hoped to present during the interview. Since this question is posed at the close of the interview, you should not elaborate for too long. Try to concisely recap a summary of the skills and attributes you bring to the company and to restate your deep interest in the company.

Sample Answer: "I just want to thank you again for taking the time to meet with me. I was really happy to receive an interview because, as I mentioned, I have for some time been working toward a goal of securing a position like the one you are offering. With the engineering skills and business experience I have gained, and project successes I have achieved in my current position, I believe I can excel in the position you are offering. I hope to have the opportunity to join your firm."

Analysis of Answer: This answer provides a very brief recap of the candidate's main theme of offering a unique blend of engineering and business experience coupled with many project successes. The positive attitude and enthusiasm of the response, combined with a restatement of the candidate's themes, will likely produce a very positive response from the interviewer.

What to Avoid: Avoid speaking for too long or sounding surprised that you were chosen for the interview. You want to sound thankful for the opportunity to interview, but you also want to sound confident in your abilities.

INDEX

Praise for *How to Interview Like a Top MBA*

"A must read! As someone who has also recruited top MBA candidates for investment banking, I unequivocally recommend *How to Interview Like a Top MBA*. It does an exceptional job of explaining what recruiters at the most sought-after corporations look for when deciding whom they should hire. Easy to read and very well organized, Dr. Leanne's book covers important aspects of the interview process and provides valuable anecdotes. Readers will find the '100 Tough Questions and How to Answer Them' particularly useful. I wish I had had this book as a resource when I was interviewing for a job years ago."

—YAHPHEN YVONNE CHANG
Columbia University and Oxford University graduate
Vice President, Debt Capital Markets—Investment Banking Group
BMO Nesbitt Burns Inc.

"Dr. Leanne's *How to Interview Like a Top MBA* has codified the nuances of landing a job in a way that I—a former recruiter for McKinsey & Co. who currently hires for my Venture Capital Firm and, at the Board Level, selects senior management in portfolio companies—find extremely compelling. I highly recommend *How to Interview Like a Top MBA!*"

—DALE LEFEBVRE
MIT graduate, Harvard Business School and Harvard Law School graduate
Former McKinsey & Company Consultant
Managing Partner, Pharos Capital